Debating Points

Debating Points:
Contemporary Social Issues Series

Henry L. Tischler, Series Editor

Debating Points:
Race and Ethnic Relations

Henry L. Tischler, Editor
Framingham State College

Prentice Hall, Upper Saddle River, New Jersey 07458

Library of Congress Cataloging-in-Publication Data

Debating points: race and ethnic relations/Henry L. Tischler, editor.
    p. cm.—(Debating points—contemporary social issues)
    Includes bibliographical references.
    ISBN 0-13-799925-9
    1. United States—Race relations. 2. United States—Ethnic relations. I. Title: Race and
ethnic relations. II. Tischler, Henry L. III. Series.

E184.A1 D285 2000
305.8'00973—dc21
                                              99-048463

Editorial director: Charlyce Jones Owen
Editor in chief: Nancy Roberts
Managing editor: Sharon Chambliss
Marketing manager: Christopher DeJohn
Editorial/production supervision: Kari Callaghan Mazzola
Electronic page makeup: Kari Callaghan Mazzola
Interior design: John P. Mazzola
Cover director: Jayne Conte
Cover design: Joe Sengotta
Buyer: Mary Ann Gloriande

This book was set in 10/12 Meridien by Big Sky Composition
and was printed and bound by Courier Companies, Inc.
The cover was printed by Phoenix Color Corp.

Printed in the United States of America
10 9 8 7 6 5 4 3 2

ISBN 0-13-799925-9

PRENTICE-HALL INTERNATIONAL (UK) LIMITED, *London*
PRENTICE-HALL OF AUSTRALIA PTY. LIMITED, *Sydney*
PRENTICE-HALL CANADA INC., *Toronto*
PRENTICE-HALL HISPANOAMERICANA, S.A., *Mexico*
PRENTICE-HALL OF INDIA PRIVATE LIMITED, *New Delhi*
PRENTICE-HALL OF JAPAN, INC., *Tokyo*
PEARSON EDUCATION ASIA PTE. LTD., *Singapore*
EDITORA PRENTICE-HALL DO BRASIL, LTDA., *Rio de Janeiro*

Contents

v

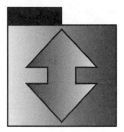

Preface

The *Debating Points: Contemporary Social Issues* series can be used to teach critical thinking, encourage student participation, and stimulate class discussion. Each book in the series is designed to provide readers with well-developed, carefully considered, and clearly written opposing viewpoints on a wide range of issues. A guiding principle in the selection of the issues for all *Debating Points* books is that they be easily understood and relevant to the backgrounds and interests of the students. Each issue within each book is self-contained and may be assigned according to the individual instructor's preferences or the dictates of classroom time.

The debate format used in each book in the *Debating Points* series helps students to understand the significance of the principles, concepts, and theories they are learning in class. It encourages students to apply critical thinking techniques to various opinions and statements. Students will see that some issues do not have "right" or "wrong" answers, and that it is important to grasp the different points of view in order to gain a fuller understanding of the issue. The purpose of the debate format is to stimulate interest in the subject matter and to encourage the application of concepts and ideas. The "yes" and "no" essays have been selected to reflect a variety of ideological viewpoints and have been edited to present the views in a concise and interesting manner. The authors of the essays have been chosen because they are creditable scholars or commentators who are respected in their fields.

In this first book in the *Debating Points* series—*Debating Points: Race and Ethnic Relations*—each issue section begins with an introduction that sets the stage for the debate by putting the issue into the context of a larger social science discussion and providing a brief description of the "yes" and "no" articles and their authors. Each issue section concludes with a list of key websites that students can research for further information on the issue. These websites have been chosen to reflect the diversity of views presented in the readings. With the advent of new communication technologies, and the growing awareness of the World Wide Web, students are being exposed more frequently to differing viewpoints and sometimes questionable information. In order to process this information effectively, students are going to have to rely on their critical thinking skills. Combining the issue articles with corresponding websites allows students to continue to explore the issues for a fuller understanding.

Many instructors have recognized the importance of applying the material that has been discussed in the classroom. The *Debating Points* series encourages students to critically evaluate the utility of various theoretical perspectives. The push is on for educators to help students strengthen their critical thinking skills. The books in the *Debating Points* series are excellent tools for teaching critical thinking in that they expose students to a variety of viewpoints and strongly argued positions related to their field of study.

Henry L. Tischler

About the Contributors

WALTER E. WILLIAMS is the John M. Olin Distinguished Professor of Economics at George Mason University. He is the author of over sixty books and articles, and his work has appeared in scholarly journals as well as popular publications. His most recent book is *More Liberty Means Less Government: Our Founders Knew This Well.*

NATHAN GLAZER is professor emeritus at the Graduate School of Education, Harvard University. He is the co-editor of the journal *The Public Interest,* as well as a contributing editor of *The New Republic.* Glazer is a leading authority on issues of race, immigration, urban development, and social policy in the United States. His books include *We Are All Multiculturalists Now* and *Beyond the Melting Pot* (with Daniel Patrick Moynihan).

GEORGE J. BORJAS is the Pforzheimer Professor of Public Policy at the John F. Kennedy School of Government, Harvard University, and a Research Associate at the National Bureau of Economic Research. He is the author of several books, including *Wage Policy in the Federal Bureaucracy; Friends or Strangers: The Impact of Immigrants on the U.S. Economy;* and *Labor Economics.* He has also written more than a hundred articles in books and scholarly journals.

ROBERTO SURO is a journalist who has worked at *Time,* the *New York Times,* and the *Washington Post,* where he is currently the deputy national editor. He is the author of *Strangers among Us: How Immigration Is Transforming America.*

CHARLES MURRAY is the Bradley Fellow at the American Enterprise Institute. He first came to national attention with *Losing Ground: American Social Policy 1950–1980,* a controversial analysis of the reforms of the 1960s. In 1994, he and the late Richard J. Herrnstein published *The Bell Curve: Intelligence and*

Class Structure in American Life, one of the most widely debated works of social science in recent decades. His latest book is *What It Means to Be a Libertarian* (1997).

HOWARD GARDNER is a professor of education and co-director of Project Zero at the Harvard Graduate School of Education, and adjunct professor of neurology at the Boston University School of Medicine. He is the author of seventeen books, including *Frames of Mind*; *Art, Mind, and Brain*; *The Unschooled Mind*; and *Leading Minds*. Gardner is best known for his theory of multiple intelligences, which holds that every human possesses several distinct intellectual faculties (rather than a singe trait called "intelligence"), each with its own way of developing and operating.

SHELDON RICHMAN is senior fellow at The Future of Freedom Foundation in Fairfax, Virginia. He is the author of *Your Money or Your Life: Why We Must Abolish the Income Tax*. His first book, *Separating School and State: How to Liberate America's Families*, is the leading book on educational liberty in the libertarian movement. He formerly was senior editor at the Cato Institute and the Institute for Humane Studies at George Mason University.

BARRY MCLAUGHLIN is a faculty member of the Psychology Board of Studies at the University of California, Santa Cruz. He is the author of various books and articles on such topics as applied psycholinguistics, second-language learning, reading, and social psychology of communication.

LEORA NEAL is the Executive Director of the New York Chapter of the Association of Black Social Workers.

RANDALL KENNEDY is a professor at Harvard Law School. He was a law clerk for Justice Thurgood Marshall of the Supreme Court of the United States. He is editor of *Reconstruction* and writes frequently on racial matters in law journals and general publications, including *The New Republic*, *Time*, the *Boston Globe*, and the *Wall Street Journal*.

ORLANDO PATTERSON is the John Cowles professor of sociology at Harvard University. Born in Jamaica, he served as special advisor for social policy and development to the Jamaican prime minister. His book *Freedom in the Making of Western Culture* won the 1991 National Book Award. He has also published three novels.

CHARLES R. LAWRENCE III and MARI J. MATSUDA are husband and wife and are both law professors at Georgetown University. They are leading voices on race issues and are frequent guests on television and radio programs. They are also the authors of *Words That Wound: Critical Race Theory, Assaultive Speech, and the First Amendment*.

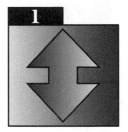

Have Affirmative Action Programs Outlived Their Usefulness?

The Civil Rights Act, with its sweeping antidiscrimination provisions, was signed into law in July of 1964. The hope was that this law would narrow the vast socioeconomic gap between the races.

That same year Daniel Patrick Moynihan, then assistant secretary of labor and future senator, wrote *The Negro Family: A Case for National Action.* Moynihan noted that progress had been made in giving black Americans full recognition of their civil rights, but he warned that this achievement was not cause for complacency because a new crisis was looming. Unless equal opportunity meant "roughly equal results," blacks would become frustrated and not feel a part of American society. The three centuries of slavery and its unimaginable treatment meant that blacks could not compete on equal terms. A new approach was needed.

Later that year, following on this theme, then President Lyndon Johnson noted, "You do not take a person who, for years, has been hobbled by chains and liberate him, bring him up to the starting line in a race and then say, 'you are free to compete.'" It was not enough just to open the gates of opportunity; all citizens also had to have the ability to walk through those gates, Johnson noted. "Equality as a fact and as a result" should be the goal.

Johnson's September 1965 Executive Order 11246 directed companies supplying goods and services to the federal government to "take affirmative action to ensure that minority applicants are employed." At the time, that meant aggressive recruitment—making extra efforts to locate black talent that had been overlooked and to give that talent the chance to develop.

Soon, concern that these policies were not working as quickly as was hoped led to the second meaning of affirmative action, one which emphasized equality of result for groups, and assumed that the best way to improve the situation of blacks was through quotas or special preferences.

1

Ironically, affirmative action quotas were first introduced in 1969 by the Nixon administration. George Shultz, Nixon's first secretary of labor, issued an administrative order that set hiring quotas for workers in the Philadelphia construction industry, an area in which employers and unions were cooperating to keep blacks out. The policy was soon extended to other cities. Other Nixon officeholders pressed similar programs with regard to faculty and students in higher education.

From these beginnings the various programs that exist today in many areas of American business and academia emerged.

Public opinion polls of whites have shown that they are opposed to preferential treatment and affirmative action. The opposition to affirmative action does not necessarily mean that whites think blacks have attained equality or that the government should not outlaw discrimination. Poll data reveals that on the central issues involving racial discrimination and Jim Crow practices, the American public is strongly against discrimination. The general agreement dissolves, however, when compulsory integration and quotas are involved. Many people oppose such efforts, not because they oppose racial equality but because they feel these measures violate their individual freedom. Most Americans do approve of concrete federal programs to help the disadvantaged and combat racial discrimination. Given a choice, however, between government intervention to solve social problems and "leaving people on their own" to work out their problems for themselves, the public tends to choose the latter (Lipset 1995).

Walter E. Williams, in "Affirmative Action Can't Be Mended," argues that affirmative action is a violation of justice and fair play, as well as racially polarizing. It is also, he says, a poor cover-up for the real work that needs to be done. Affirmative action focuses our attention on discrimination instead of trying to correct such factors as fraudulent education, family disintegration, and hostile economic climates in black neighborhoods.

Nathan Glazer, on the other hand, in his article "In Defense of Preference," argues that we have to continue racial preferences for blacks: first, because the United States has a special obligation to blacks that has not been fully discharged; second, because the strict application of the principle of qualifications would send a message of despair to many blacks, a message that the nation is indifferent to their difficulties and problems.

Affirmative Action Can't Be Mended

Walter E.
Williams

For the last several decades, affirmative action has been the basic component of the civil rights agenda. But affirmative action, in the form of racial
preferences, has worn out its political welcome. In Gallup Polls, between
1987 and 1990, people were asked if they agreed with the statement: "We
should make every effort to improve the position of blacks and other
minorities even if it means giving them preferential treatment." More than
70 percent of the respondents opposed preferential treatment while only 24
percent supported it. Among blacks, 66 percent opposed preferential treatment and 32 percent supported it (Lipset 1992: 66–69).

The rejection of racial preferences by the broad public and increasingly by the Supreme Court has been partially recognized by even supporters
of affirmative action. While they have not forsaken their goals, they have
begun to distance themselves from some of the language of affirmative
action. Thus, many business, government, and university affirmative action
offices have been renamed "equity offices." Racial preferences are increasingly referred to as "diversity multiculturalism." What is it about affirmative
action that gives rise to its contentiousness?

...

Yesteryear civil rights organizations fought against the use of race in
hiring, access to public schools, and university admissions. Today, civil rights
organizations fight for the use of race in hiring, access to public schools, and
university admissions. Yesteryear, civil rights organizations fought against
restricted association in the forms of racially segregated schools, libraries,
and private organizations. Today, they fight for restricted associations. They

From *Cato Journal* 17, no. 1 (spring/summer 1997). Copyright © 1997 by The Cato Institute. Reprinted with
the permission of The Cato Institute, http://www.cato.org.

use state power, not unlike the racists they fought, to enforce racial associations they deem desirable. They protest that blacks should be a certain percentage of a company's workforce or clientele, a certain percentage of a student body, and even a certain percentage of an advertiser's models.

Civil rights organizations, in their successful struggle against state-sanctioned segregation, have lost sight of what it means to be truly committed to liberty, especially the freedom of association. The true test of that commitment does not come when we allow people to be free to associate in ways we deem appropriate. The true test is when we allow people to form those voluntary associations we deem offensive. It is the same principle we apply to our commitment to free speech. What tests our commitment to free speech is our willingness to permit people the freedom to say things we find offensive.

Zero-Sum Games

...

A zero-sum game is defined as any transaction where one person's gain necessarily results in another person's loss. The simplest example of a zero-sum game is poker. A winner's gain is matched precisely by the losses of one or more persons. In this respect, the only essential difference between affirmative action and poker is that in poker participation is voluntary. Another difference is the loser is readily identifiable, a point to which I will return later.

The University of California, Berkeley's affirmative action program for blacks captures the essence of a zero-sum game. Blacks are admitted with considerably lower average SAT scores (952) than the typical white (1232) and Asian student (1254) (Sowell 1993: 144). Between UCLA and UC Berkeley, more than 2,000 white and Asian straight A students are turned away in order to provide spaces for black and Hispanic students (Lynch 1989: 163). The admissions gains by blacks are exactly matched by admissions losses by white and Asian students. Thus, any preferential treatment program results in a zero-sum game almost by definition.

More generally, government allocation of resources is a zero-sum game primarily because government has no resources of its very own. When government gives some citizens food stamps, crop subsidies, or disaster relief payments, the recipients of the largesse gain. Losers are identified by asking: Where does government acquire the resources to confer the largesse? In order for government to give to some citizens, it must through intimidation, threats, and coercion take from other citizens. Those who lose the rights to their earnings, to finance government largesse, are the losers.

Government-mandated racial preferential treatment programs produce a similar result. When government creates a special advantage for one ethnic group, it necessarily comes at the expense of other ethnic groups for whom government simultaneously creates a special disadvantage in the form of reduced alternatives. If a college or employer has X amount of positions, and R of them have been set aside for blacks or some other group, that necessarily means there are (X-R) fewer positions for which other ethnic groups might compete. At a time when there were restrictions against blacks, that operated in favor of whites, those restrictions translated into a reduced opportunity set for blacks. It is a zero-sum game independent of the race or ethnicity of the winners and losers.

...

Tentative Victim Identification

In California, voters passed the California Civil Rights Initiative of 1996 (CCRI) that says: "The state shall not discriminate against, or grant preferential treatment to, any individual or group on the basis of race, sex, color, ethnicity, or national origin in the operation of public employment, public education, or public contracting." Therefore, California public universities can no longer have preferential admission policies that include race as a factor in deciding whom to admit.

For illustrative purposes, let us pretend that CCRI had not been adopted and the UCLA School of Law accepted 108 black students as it had in 1996 and UC Berkeley accepted 75. That being the case, 83 more blacks would be accepted to UCLA Law School for the 1997–98 academic year and 61 more blacks would be accepted to UC Berkeley's Law School. Clearly, the preferential admissions program, at least in terms of being accepted to these law schools, benefits blacks. However, that benefit is not without costs. With preferential admission programs in place, both UCLA and UC Berkeley law schools would have had to turn away 144 white and Asian students, with higher academic credentials, in order to have room for black students.

In the case of UC Berkeley's preferential admissions for blacks, those whites and Asians who have significantly higher SAT scores and grades than the admitted blacks are victims of reverse discrimination. However, in the eyes of the courts, others, and possibly themselves, they are invisible victims. In other words, no one can tell for sure who among those turned away would have gained entry to UC Berkeley were it not for the preferential treatment given to blacks.

...

Affirmative Action and Supply

An important focus of affirmative action is statistical underrepresentation of different racial and ethnic groups on college and university campuses. If the percentages of blacks and Mexican-Americans, for example, are not at a level deemed appropriate by a court, administrative agency, or university administrator, racial preference programs are instituted. The inference made from the underrepresentation argument is that, in the absence of racial discrimination, groups would be represented on college campuses in proportion to their numbers in the relevant population. In making that argument, little attention is paid to the supply issue—that is, to the pool of students available that meet the standards or qualifications of the university in question.

... If blacks scoring 600 or higher on the quantitative portion of the SAT (assuming their performance on the verbal portion of the examination gave them a composite SAT score of 1200 or higher) were recruited to elite colleges and universities, there would be less than 33 black students available per university. At none of those universities would blacks be represented according to their numbers in the population.

There is no evidence that suggests that university admissions offices practice racial discrimination by turning away blacks with SAT scores of 1200 or higher. In reality, there are not enough blacks to be admitted to leading colleges and universities on the same terms as other students, such that their numbers in the campus population bears any resemblance to their numbers in the general population.

Attempts by affirmative action programs to increase the percent of blacks admitted to top schools, regardless of whether blacks match the academic characteristics of the general student body, often produce disastrous results. In order to meet affirmative action guidelines, leading colleges and universities recruit and admit black students whose academic qualifications are well below the norm for other students. For example, of the 317 black students admitted to UC Berkeley in 1985, all were admitted under affirmative action criteria rather than academic qualifications. Those students had an average SAT score of 952 compared to the national average of 900 among all students. However, their SAT scores were well below UC Berkeley's average of nearly 1200. More than 70 percent of the black students failed to graduate from UC Berkeley (Sowell 1993: 144).

...

There is no question that preferential admissions is unjust to both white and Asian students who may be qualified but are turned away to make room for less-qualified students in the "right" ethnic group. However, viewed from a solely black self-interest point of view, the question should be asked whether such affirmative action programs serve the best interests of blacks. Is there such an abundance of black students who score above the national average on the SAT, such as those admitted to UC Berkeley, that blacks as a group can afford to have those students turned into artificial failures in the name of diversity, multiculturalism, or racial justice? The affirmative action debate needs to go beyond simply an issue of whether blacks are benefited at the expense of whites. Whites and Asians who are turned away to accommodate blacks are still better off than the blacks who were admitted. After all, graduating from the university of one's second choice is preferable to flunking out of the university of one's first choice.

To the extent racial preferences in admission produce an academic mismatch of students, the critics may be unnecessarily alarmed, assuming their concern is with black students actually graduating from college. If black students who score 952 on the SAT are not admitted to UC Berkeley, that does not mean that they cannot gain admittance to one of America's 3,000 other colleges. It means that they will gain admittance to some other college where their academic characteristics will be more similar to those of their peers. There will not be as much of an academic mismatch. To the extent this is true, we may see an increase in black graduation rates. Moreover, if black students find themselves more similar to their white peers in terms of college grades and graduation honors, they are less likely to feel academically isolated and harbor feelings of low self-esteem.

Affirmative Action and Justice

Aside from any other question, we might ask what case can be made for the morality or justice of turning away more highly credentialed white and Asian students so as to be able to admit more blacks. Clearly, blacks as a group have suffered past injustices, including discrimination in college and university admissions. However, that fact does not spontaneously yield sensible policy proposals for today. The fact is that a special privilege cannot be created for one person without creating a special disadvantage for another. In the case of preferential admissions, a special privilege for black students translates into a special disadvantage for white and Asian students. Thus, we must ask what have those individual white and Asian students done to deserve punishment? Were they at all responsible for the injustices, either in the past or present, suffered by blacks? If, as so often is the case, the justification for preferential treatment is to redress past grievances, how just is it to have a policy where a black of today is helped by punishing a white of today for what a white of yesterday did to a black of yesterday? Such an idea becomes even more questionable in light of the fact that so many whites and Asians cannot trace the American part of their ancestry back as much as two or three generations.

Affirmative Action and Racial Resentment

In addition to the injustices that are a result of preferential treatment, such treatment has given rise to racial resentment where it otherwise might not exist. While few people support racial resentment and its manifestations, if one sees some of affirmative action's flagrant attacks on fairness and equality before the law, one can readily understand why resentment is on the rise.

...

Affirmative action proponents cling to the notion that racial discrimination satisfactorily explains black/white socioeconomic differences. While every vestige of racial discrimination has not been eliminated in our society, current social discrimination cannot begin to explain all that affirmative action proponents' purport it explains. Rather than focusing our attention on discrimination, a higher payoff can be realized by focusing on real factors such as fraudulent education, family disintegration, and hostile economic climates in black neighborhoods. Even if affirmative action was not a violation of justice and fair play, was not a zero-sum game, was not racially polarizing, it is a poor cover-up for the real work that needs to be done.

References

Cunico v. Pueblo School District No. 60 (1990) 917 F. 2D 431 (10th Circuit).

Eastland, T. (1996). *Ending Affirmative Action: The Case for Colorblind Justice.* New York: Basic Books.

Lipset, S. M. (1992). "Equal Chances versus Equal Results." In H. Orlans and J. O'Neill, eds. *Affirmative Action Revisited; Annuals of the American Academy of Political and Social Science* (September): 63–74.

Lynch, F. R. (1989). *Invisible Victims: White Males and the Crisis of Affirmative Action.* New York: Greenwood Press.

Roberts, P. C., and Stratton, L. M. (1995). *The Color Line: How Quotas and Privilege Destroy Democracy.* Washington, D.C.: Regnery.

Sowell, T. (1990). *Preferential Policies: An International Perspective.* New York: William Morrow.

———. (1993). *Inside American Education: The Decline, the Deception, the Dogmas.* New York: The Free Press.

United States General Accounting Office. (1995). *Efforts by the Office for Civil Rights to Resolve Asian-American Complaints.* Washington, D.C.: Government Printing Office (December).

Weiss, K. R. (1997). "UC Law Schools' New Rules Cost Minorities Spots." *Los Angeles Times,* 15 May.

Wygant v. Jackson Board of Education (1982) 546 F. Supp. 1195.

Wygant v. Jackson Board of Education (1986) 476 U.S. 267.

Nathan
Glazer

In Defense
of Preference

The battle over affirmative action today is a contest between a clear principle on the one hand and a clear reality on the other. The principle is that
ability, qualifications, and merit, independent of race, national origin, or
sex should prevail when one applies for a job or promotion, or for entry
into selective institutions for higher education, or when one bids for contracts. The reality is that strict adherence to this principle would result in
few African Americans getting jobs, admissions, and contracts. What makes
the debate so confused is that the facts that make a compelling case for
affirmative action are often obscured by the defenders of affirmative action
themselves. They have resisted acknowledging how serious the gaps are
between African Americans and others, how deep the preferences reach,
how systematic they have become. Considerably more than a mild bent in
the direction of diversity now exists, but it exists because painful facts make
it necessary if blacks are to participate in more than token numbers in some
key institutions of our society. The opponents of affirmative action can also
be faulted: They have not fully confronted the consequences that must follow from the implementation of the principle that measured ability, qualification, merit, applied without regard to color, should be our only guide.

...

The reality of this enormous gap is clearest where the tests in use are
the most objective, the most reliable, and the best validated, as in the case
of the various tests used for admission to selective institutions of higher education, for entry into elite occupations such as law and medicine, or for civil
service jobs. These tests have been developed over many years specifically
for the purpose of eliminating biases in admissions and appointments. As

From *The New Republic* 218, no. 14 (April 6, 1998). Copyright © 1998 by The New Republic, Inc. Reprinted
with the permission of The New Republic.

defenders of affirmative action often point out, paper-and-pencil tests of information, reading comprehension, vocabulary, reasoning, and the like are not perfect indicators of individual ability. But they are the best measures we have for success in college and professional schools, which, after all, require just the skills the tests measure. And the tests can clearly differentiate the literate teacher from the illiterate one or the policeman who can make out a coherent arrest report from one who cannot.

···

There is no way of getting around this reality. Perhaps the tests are irrelevant to success in college? That cannot be sustained. They have been improved and revised over decades and predict achievement in college better than any alternative. Some of the revisions have been carried out in a near-desperate effort to exclude items which would discriminate against blacks. Some institutions have decided they will not use the tests, not because they are invalid per se, but because they pose a barrier to the increased admission of black students. Nor would emphasizing other admissions criteria, such as high school grades, make a radical difference. In any case, there is considerable value to a uniform national standard, given the enormous differences among high schools.

Do qualifications at the time of admission matter? Isn't the important thing what the institutions manage to do with those they admit? If they graduate, are they not qualified? Yes, but many do not graduate. Two or three times as many African American students as white students drop out before graduation. And the tests for admission to graduate schools show the same radical disparities between blacks and others. Are there not also preferences for athletes, children of alumni, students gifted in some particular respect? Yes, but except for athletes, the disparities in academic aptitude that result from such preferences are not nearly as substantial as those which must be elided in order to reach target figures for black students. Can we not substitute for the tests other factors—such as the poverty and other hardships students have overcome to reach the point of applying to college? This might keep up the number of African Americans, but not by much, if the studies are to be believed. A good number of white and Asian applicants would also benefit from such "class-based" affirmative action.

···

How, then, should we respond to this undeniable reality? The opponents of affirmative action say, "Let standards prevail whatever the result." So what if black students are reduced to two percent of our selective and elite student bodies? Those who gain entry will know that they are properly qualified for entry, that they have been selected without discrimination, and their classmates will know it too. The result will actually be improved race relations and a continuance of the improvements we have seen in black performance in recent decades. Fifteen years from now, perhaps three or four percent of students in the top schools will be black. Until then, blacks can go to less competitive institutions of higher education, perhaps gaining greater advantage from their education in so doing. And, meanwhile, let us improve elementary and high school education—as we have been trying to do for the last 15 years or more.

Yet we cannot be quite so cavalier about the impact on public opinion—black and white—of a radical reduction in the number of black students at the Harvards, the Berkeleys, and the Amhersts. These institutions have become, for better or worse, the gateways to prominence, privilege, wealth, and power in American society. To admit blacks under affirmative action no doubt undermines the American meritocracy, but to exclude blacks from them by abolishing affirmative action would undermine the legitimacy of American democracy.

My argument is rooted in history. African Americans—and the struggle for their full and fair inclusion in U.S. society—have been a part of American history from the beginning. Our Constitution took special—but grossly unfair—account of their status, our greatest war was fought over their status, and our most important constitutional amendments were adopted because of the need to right past wrongs done to them. And, amid the civil rights revolution of the 1960s, affirmative action was instituted to compensate for the damage done to black achievement and life chances by almost 400 years of slavery, followed by state-sanctioned discrimination and massive prejudice.

Yet, today, a vast gulf of difference persists between the educational and occupational status of blacks and whites, a gulf that encompasses statistical measures of wealth, residential segregation, and social relationships with other Americans. Thirty years ago, with the passage of the great civil rights laws, one could have reasonably expected—as I did—that all would be set right by now. But today, even after taking account of substantial progress and change, it is borne upon us how continuous, rooted, and substantial the differences between African Americans and other Americans remain.

The judgment of the elites who support affirmative action—the college presidents and trustees, the religious leaders, the corporate executives—and the judgment even of many of those who oppose it but hesitate to act against it—the Republican leaders in Congress, for example—is that the banning of preference would be bad for the country. I agree. Not that everyone's motives are entirely admirable; many conservative congressmen, for example, are simply afraid of being portrayed as racists even if their opposition to affirmative action is based on a sincere desire to support meritocratic principle. The college presidents who support affirmative action, under the fashionable mantra of diversity, also undoubtedly fear the student demonstrations that would occur if they were to speak out against preferences.

But there are also good-faith motives in this stand, and there is something behind the argument for diversity. What kind of institutions of higher education would we have if blacks suddenly dropped from six or seven percent of enrollment to one or two percent? The presence of blacks, in classes in social studies and the humanities, immediately introduces another tone, another range of questions (often to the discomfort of black students who do not want this representational burden placed upon them). The tone may be one of embarrassment and hesitation and self-censorship among whites (students and faculty). But must we not all learn how to face these questions together with our fellow citizens? We should not be able to escape from this embarrassment by the reduction of black students to minuscule numbers.

...

... But I believe the main reasons we have to continue racial preferences for blacks are, first, because this country has a special obligation to blacks that has not been fully discharged, and second, because strict application of the principle of qualification would send a message of despair to many blacks, a message that the nation is indifferent to their difficulties and problems.

...

Whatever the case one may make in general for affirmative action, many difficult issues remain: What kind, to what extent, how long, imposed by whom, by what decision-making process? It is important to bear in mind that affirmative action in higher education admissions is, for the most part, a policy that has been chosen (albeit sometimes under political pressure) by the institutions themselves....

...

We should retain the freedom of institutions of higher and profession-al education to make these determinations for themselves. As we know, they would almost all make room for a larger percentage of black students than would otherwise qualify. This is what these institutions do today. They defend what they do with the argument that diversity is a good thing. I think what they really mean is that a large segment of the American popu-lation, significant not only demographically but historically and politically and morally, cannot be so thoroughly excluded. I agree with them.

...

... Preference is no final answer (just as the elimination of preference is no final answer). It is rather what is necessary to respond to the reality that, for some years to come, yes, we are still two nations, and both nations must participate in the society to some reasonable degree.

Fortunately, those two nations, by and large, want to become more united. The United States is not Canada or Bosnia, Lebanon or Malaysia. But, for the foreseeable future, the strict use of certain generally reasonable tests as a benchmark criterion for admissions would mean the de facto exclusion of one of the two nations from a key institutional system of the society, high-er education. Higher education's governing principle is qualification—merit. Should it make room for another and quite different principle, equal partic-ipation? The latter should never become dominant. Racial proportional rep-resentation would be a disaster. But basically the answer is yes—the principle of equal participation can and should be given some role. This decision has costs. But the alternative is too grim to contemplate.

KEY WEBSITES

AAD PROJECT

The Affirmative Action and Diversity Project is a web page designed to stimulate discussion and debate about affirmative action and diversity issues regarding culture, gender, race, and color. It provides links to pending court cases, state and federal legislation, and an annotated bibliography.
http://humanitas.ucsb.edu/aa.html

AAUP—DIVERSITY AND AFFIRMATIVE ACTION IN HIGHER EDUCATION

This website, compiled by the American Association of University Professors, contains essays, articles, and background information about affirmative action in higher education.
http://www.aaup.org/aacntnts.htm

AFFACT WEB: HOME PAGE OF THE AMERICAN ASSOCIATION FOR AFFIRMATIVE ACTION (AAAA)

AffAct Web contains information, news, and Web links related to Affirmative Action issues and Congress, federal agencies, the White House, the courts, and various states.
http://www.affirmativeaction.org/

AFFIRMATIVE ACTION: MYTHS VS. FACTS

This website, compiled by the Coalition against Bigotry and Bias, a Washington-state-based organization, contains statistics and information about affirmative action.
http://www.bbcc.ctc.edu/~webb/cabb.htm

AFFIRMATIVE ACTION WEB RESOURCES

This website provides links to dozens of websites, online newspaper and journal articles, and university policies and programs prepared by the Affirmative Action and Diversity Project at the University of California at Santa Barbara.
http://humanitas.ucsb.edu/projects/aa/pages/a-action.htmltop

AMERICANS AGAINST DISCRIMINATION AND PREFERENCES

This group works for the abolition of racial and gender discrimination and preferences at the local, state, and federal levels, along the lines established by California's Proposition 209. The website includes daily updates of links to news articles on affirmative action and race.
http://www.aadap.org/

AMERICANS UNITED FOR AFFIRMATIVE ACTION

Americans United for Affirmative Action is a national, nonprofit organization committed to educating the public on the importance of maintaining affirmative action programs and the principles of equal opportunity in employment and education.
http://www.auaa.org/index.html

U.S. SUPREME COURT SYLLABI: AFFIRMATIVE ACTION

This website, compiled by Cornell University's Legal Information Institute, provides a searchable index to identify affirmative action cases heard by the Supreme Court.
http://www4.law.cornell.edu/cgi-bin/fx?DB=SupctSyllabi&
   TOPDOC=0&P=affirmative+action

Are Greater Restrictions on Immigration Needed?

The inscription on New York's Statue of Liberty (written by Emma Lazarus in 1883) invites the rest of the world to "give us your tired, your poor ... the wretched refuse of your teeming shore." Europe, the invitation implied, was old, tired, and crowded. For immigrants, the statue's message offered a chance for a better life. For the United States, the immigrants provided a fresh influx of new life needed to build and develop the nation. Immigration was seen as a beneficial arrangement all around.

Throughout our history there have always been people who questioned whether America really had the seemingly infinite space and opportunities implied by the inscription on the Statue of Liberty. Today is no different, and many people are concerned about problems such as job insecurity, diminishing resources, and mounting social tensions—concerns that suggest a growing sensitivity to limits and to the idea that there may now be too many people vying to share in the resources of the United States.

While this shift to a less hopeful national mood may account in part for recent high levels of contentiousness surrounding the immigration issue, our history shows that immigration has always been an incendiary issue, even during bygone eras of expansion and optimism.

In the article "The New Economics of Immigration," George J. Borjas points out that because of changes in our immigration policy initiated in 1965 the number of immigrants coming to the country each year has been rising steadily. Whereas about 250,000 immigrants came to the United States each year in the 1950s, now the number is closer to 900,000. On top of that, there are at least 300,000 illegal immigrants entering the country each year.

The countries from which immigrants are coming have also changed. From the beginning of the United States until the 1950s the vast majority of immigrants were of European origin. Now most immigrants come from Latin America and Asia.

Borjas believes that something must be done quickly to address the difficult social and economic conditions that are likely to result from our current immigration policy. Ignoring the problem merely postpones the inevitable day of reckoning, he warns.

Roberto Suro, in "Watching America's Door," points out that even with the political heat and rhetoric that it generates, immigration does not lend itself to quick fixes. The nation is currently in the midst of a mature migration that began three decades ago with changes in U.S. immigration laws, labor force demands, and foreign policies. Any attempt to manage such a powerful demographic force will require a consistent, long-term effort involving many steps and a great deal of flexibility.

The New Economics of Immigration
Affluent Americans Gain; Poor Americans Lose

George J.
Borjas

... There have been two major shifts in immigration policy in this century. In the twenties the United States began to limit the number of immigrants admitted and established the national-origins quota system, an allocation scheme that awarded entry visas mainly on the basis of national origin and that favored Germany and the United Kingdom. This system was repealed in 1965, and family reunification became the central goal of immigration policy, with entry visas being awarded mainly to applicants who had relatives already residing in the United States.

The social, demographic, and economic changes initiated by the 1965 legislation have been truly historic. The number of immigrants began to rise rapidly. As recently as the 1950s only about 250,000 immigrants entered the country annually; by the 1990s the United States was admitting more than 800,000 legal immigrants a year, and some 300,000 aliens entered and stayed in the country illegally. The 1965 legislation also led to a momentous shift in the ethnic composition of the population. Although people of European origin dominated the immigrant flow from the country's founding until the 1950s, only about 10 percent of those admitted in the 1980s were of European origin. It is now estimated that non-Hispanic whites may form a minority of the population soon after 2050. More troubling is that immigration has been linked to the increase in income inequality observed since the 1980s, and to an increase in the costs of maintaining the programs that make up the welfare state.

...

From *The Atlantic Monthly* 278, no. 5 (November 1996). Copyright © 1996 by George J. Borjas. Reprinted with the permission of the author.

A Formula for Admission

Every immigration policy must resolve two distinct issues: how many immigrants the country should admit, and what kinds of people they should be.

It is useful to view immigration policy as a formula that gives points to visa applicants on the basis of various characteristics and then sets a passing grade. The variables in the formula determine what kinds of people will be let into the country, and the passing grade determines how many will be let into the country. Current policy uses a formula that has one overriding variable: whether the visa applicant has a family member already residing in the United States. An applicant who has a relative in the country gets 100 points, passes the test, and is admitted. An applicant who does not gets 0 points, fails the test, and cannot immigrate legally.

...

What Have We Learned?

The academic literature investigating the economic impact of immigration on the United States has grown rapidly in the past decade. The assumptions that long dominated discussion of the costs and benefits of immigration were replaced during the 1980s by a number of new questions, issues, and perceptions.

Consider the received wisdom of the early 1980s. The studies available suggested that even though immigrants arrived at an economic disadvantage, their opportunities improved rapidly over time. Within a decade or two of immigrants' arrival their earnings would overtake the earnings of natives of comparable socioeconomic background. The evidence also suggested that immigrants did no harm to native employment opportunities, and were less likely to receive welfare assistance than natives. Finally, the children of immigrants were even more successful than their parents. The empirical evidence, therefore, painted a very optimistic picture of the contribution that immigrants made to the American economy.

In the past ten years this picture has altered radically. New research has established a number of points.

- The relative skills of successive immigrant waves have declined over much of the postwar period. In 1970, for example, the latest immigrant arrivals on average had 0.4 fewer years of schooling and earned 17 percent less than natives. By 1990 the most recently arrived immigrants had 1.3 fewer years of schooling and earned 32 percent less than natives.

- Because the newest immigrant waves start out at such an economic disadvantage, and because the rate of economic assimilation is not very rapid, the earnings of the newest arrivals may never reach parity with the earnings of natives. Recent arrivals will probably earn 20 percent less than natives throughout much of their working lives.

- The large-scale migration of less-skilled workers has done harm to the economic opportunities of less-skilled natives. Immigration may account for perhaps a third of the recent decline in the relative wages of less-educated native workers.

- The new immigrants are more likely to receive welfare assistance than earlier immigrants, and also more likely to do so than natives: 21 percent of immigrant households participate in some means-tested social-assistance program (such as cash benefits, Medicaid, or food stamps), as compared with 14 percent of native households.

- The increasing welfare dependency in the immigrant population suggests that immigration may create a substantial fiscal burden on the most-affected localities and states.

- There are economic benefits to be gained from immigration. These arise because certain skills that immigrants bring into the country complement those of the native population. However, these economic benefits are small—perhaps on the order of $7 billion annually.

- There exists a strong correlation between the skills of immigrants and the skills of their American-born children, so that the huge skill differentials observed among today's foreign-born groups will almost certainly become tomorrow's differences among American-born ethnic groups. In effect, immigration has set the stage for sizable ethnic differences in skills and socioeconomic outcomes, which are sure to be the focus of intense attention in the next century.

- The United States is only beginning to observe the economic consequences of the historic changes in the numbers, national origins, and skills of immigrants admitted over the past three decades. Regardless of how immigration policy changes in the near future, we have already set in motion circumstances that will surely alter the economic prospects of native workers and the costs of social-insurance programs not only in our generation but for our children and grandchildren as well.

...

How Many and Whom Should We Admit?

In principle, we should admit immigrants whenever their economic contribution (to native well-being) will exceed the costs of providing social services to them. We are not, though, in a position to make this calculation with any reasonable degree of confidence. In fact, no mainstream study has ever attempted to suggest, purely on the basis of the empirical evidence, how many immigrants should be admitted.

...

Although we do not know how many immigrants to admit, simple economics and common sense suggest that the magic number should not be an immutable constant regardless of economic conditions in the United States. A good case can be made for linking immigration to the business cycle: Admit more immigrants when the economy is strong and the unemployment rate is low, and cut back on immigration when the economy is weak and the unemployment rate is high.

Economic research also suggests that the United States may be better off if its policy of awarding entry visas favors skilled workers. Skilled immigrants earn more than less-skilled immigrants, and hence pay more in taxes, and they are less likely to use welfare and other social services.

Depending on how the skills of immigrants compare with the skills of natives, immigrants also affect the productivity of the native work force and of native-owned companies. Skilled native workers, for example, have much to gain when less-skilled workers enter the United States: They can devote all their efforts to jobs that use their skills effectively while immigrants provide cheap labor for service jobs. These gains, however, come at a cost. The jobs of less-skilled natives are now at risk, and these natives will suffer a reduction in their earnings. Nonetheless, it does not seem far-fetched to assume that the American work force, particularly in comparison with the work forces of many source countries, is composed primarily of skilled workers. Thus the typical American worker would seem to gain from unskilled immigration.

...

Distributional issues drive the political debate over many social policies, and immigration policy is no exception. The debate over immigration policy is not a debate over whether the entire country is made better off by immigration—the gains from immigration seem much too small, and could even be outweighed by the costs of providing increased social services. Immigration changes how the economic pie is sliced up—and this fact goes a long way toward explaining why the debate over how many and what kinds of immigrants to admit is best viewed as a tug-of-war between those who gain from immigration and those who lose from it.

History has taught us that immigration policy changes rarely, but when it does, it changes drastically. Can economic research play a role in finding a better policy? I believe it can, but there are dangers ahead. Although the pendulum seems to be swinging to the restrictionist side (with ever louder calls for a complete closing of our borders), a greater danger to the national interest may be the few economic groups that gain much from immigration. They seem indifferent to the costs that immigration imposes on other segments of society, and they have considerable financial incentives to keep the current policy in place. The harmful effects of immigration will not go away simply because some people do not wish to see them. In the short run these groups may simply delay the day of reckoning. Their potential long-run impact, however, is much more perilous: The longer the delay, the greater the chances that when immigration policy finally changes, it will undergo a seismic shift—one that, as in the twenties, may come close to shutting down the border and preventing Americans from enjoying the benefits that a well-designed immigration policy can bestow on the United States.

Watching America's Door
The Immigration Backlash and the New Policy Debate

Roberto
Suro

Despite the political heat and rhetoric that it generates, immigration does not lend itself to quick fixes....

The nation is currently in the midst of a mature migration that began three decades ago with changes in U.S. immigration laws, labor force demands, and foreign policies. By the 1990s, immigration was adding more than a million people a year to the U.S. population. Immigration to the United States now represents a huge and well-established demographic force with its own dynamic. The contemporary immigration flow involves millions of people in dozens of countries who have developed familial and economic connections to the United States—connections that have created the momentum for future influxes. Having encouraged the development of this human flow over the past thirty years, the United States will be hard-pressed to change its direction with a one-shot overhaul of immigration laws. Any attempt to manage such a powerful demographic force will require a consistent, long-term effort involving many steps and a great deal of flexibility.

To begin with, a new perspective is needed from which to debate immigration policies. Currently the issue is viewed as the challenge of enforcing sovereignty and controlling a flow of people that emanates from abroad. But the real challenge is to make immigration work to the nation's benefit, to understand how it relates to a variety of social and economic dynamics, to establish a set of goals and priorities, and then try to tailor the flow to these objectives. People can and will disagree over how much immigration is beneficial and how much is too much....

Throughout the early 1990s the nation's television screens were filled with images that reinforced fears that the United States was the helpless target of millions of unwanted migrants from all over the world. A nation that had been protected by two oceans from the worst ravages of war for so long suddenly saw itself as vulnerable to a different kind of invasion.

This previously unthinkable sense of geographic vulnerability may be one of the most subtle and potent sources of the anxiety caused by immigration. And the perceived threat was massive and widespread. The "entire Third World" became an important demographic concept as the immigration backlash developed. Some advocates of restrictive policies proclaimed the existence of a veritable subspecies of human beings with distinct characteristics: They lived primarily in warm climates, they were not white, they were poor and badly educated, they reproduced so quickly that they existed in infinite supply, and they all wanted to come to the United States....

...

Virtually all proposals for restriction are based on a simple construct: Immigration pressures are generated in the world outside our borders, and immigration policies must serve as a barrier that withstands that pressure and controls access to the nation. This assumption is not advanced just by restrictionists. Until recently, it also informed a great deal of academic research and the advocacy of those who favor high levels of immigration.

Throughout the mid-1990s the debate has been between those who feel that current levels of immigration are good for the country or at worst do no harm and those who feel the numbers should come down. Either way the basic principle is the same: The human pressure is on the outside, and immigration policy is the control valve. In fact, this premise is incorrect and deceptive.

First, there is no undifferentiated demographic pressure that characterizes immigration. People come to the United States from relatively few specific places, not equally from the whole of the world. Each of these flows has developed out of its own history and has unique characteristics in terms of the kinds of people who come, where in the sending society they come from, and where they end up in the United States. Rather than a uniform pressure from outside, overall immigration is a collection of thousands of different individual flows. Rather than water pouring from a faucet depending on how far it is opened, immigration is like electricity coming through a bundle of multicolored wires, each connecting with its own circuitry.

Second, the United States is not merely a passive receptor. It does not exercise an undifferentiated appeal for all persons living in less affluent nations. Instead, a variety of social and economic forces within the United States, such as job opportunities in a given sector of the economy, attract particular types of immigrants. The United States itself also creates circumstances that stimulate migrations. For example, the long-term presence of American military forces in the Philippines and Korea has helped generate a larger flow from those countries than from other Asian nations. And in some situations, U.S. government policies have been the most important stimulus of the influx. Mexican farmworkers, Hmong tribesmen from Laos, and Filipino nurses each represent flows instigated specifically by U.S. policies.

However, as the new debate over immigration developed in the mid-1990s most of the discussion continued to reflect these twin misapprehensions: that immigration is the result of a global demographic pressure and that the role of U.S. immigration policy is to act as a spigot regulating how much of that mass of humanity should be allowed to enter at a time.

These erroneous perceptions are deeply rooted in the history of U.S. immigration policies. Beginning with the Asian exclusion laws of the late nineteenth century, the United States attempted to control immigration with policies aimed at specific racial and ethnic groups. The intellectual basis for these policies was the thought that humanity could be divided into races and cultures with immutable characteristics and judged according to their desirability. (The domestic counterpart of this approach was Jim Crow segregation.) It produced widely accepted judgments that people of many nationalities were simply incapable of operating in a democracy and a free market economy. This trend in policymaking culminated with the National Origins Act of 1924 and its highly restrictive system of country-specific quotas.

When the Immigration Act of 1965 overturned that system, President Lyndon B. Johnson said, "Every American can be proud today because we have finally eliminated the cruel and unjust national origins system from the immigration policy of the United States. We have righted a long-standing wrong. So today, any man, anywhere in the world can hope to begin a new life of freedom and a new life of greater opportunity in the United States. No longer will his color or his religion or his nationality be a barrier to him."

… By rejecting as racist the notion that immigrants of certain nationalities are undesirable, the United States adopted a perspective that viewed all prospective immigrants as equals. The new policy was born out of the logic of the civil rights movement and a moral imperative to avoid even the semblance of discrimination.…

…

Since the early days of this century, U.S. immigration law has included one provision or another designed to bar foreigners who are likely to become dependent on tax-supported social services. Although it may be the single most enduring element of immigration policy, the goal of preventing poor immigrants from becoming a drain on public resources received especially close attention in the mid-1990s.

…

The current emphasis on immigrant use of public services and benefits reflects a broader anxiety about the unharnessed growth of entitlement programs and concerns about the large number of immigrants who come to the

United States poor and stay poor. But it also reflects an evolution in the immigrant population itself.

Young adults generally make up a disproportionately large part of an immigrant flow. This has been true across the ages because they are the travelers and adventurers in any society. Young adults tend to migrate alone rather than in family units, and single males often make up a large share of an immigrant population, especially in the early stages of a migration. For example, the 1994 Census survey found that nearly half of the foreign born who had entered the country since 1990 were between the ages of eighteen and thirty-four, compared with about a quarter of the general population in the same age range. Among the immigrants who came in the 1980s, men outnumbered women by 11 percent, although by the 1990s the gender ratio had nearly evened out.

Young adults do not tend to remain alone under any circumstances, and the difficulties of immigration encourage the formation of strong household structures and extended families. The immigrant flow may begin with single young people, but it does not remain that way.

...

Single young adults are workers. They generally contribute to society and do not ask for much back. Families, on the other hand, usually have children who contribute nothing materially but require a great deal in the way of health and education. And once families are established, they often include the elderly of the previous generation, who also present substantial costs for needed care.

A mature migration involves very different policy challenges from an immigrant flow so fresh that it is characterized mainly by low-cost young adults. The current wave of immigration continues to bring a large proportion of people who are in the most productive phase of their lives, but the foreign-born population has been building for thirty years, and with considerable intensity for fifteen years. There is now a sizable group of people who have been in the United States long enough to form families and reach the point where their costs to society are on the rise. This has put immigrants' use of social benefits on the table as a major policy issue.

...

A mature migration presents challenges beyond the realm of social benefits and the manner in which newcomers become integrated into American society. The initial step of simply determining how many immigrants to let into the country is different when a government is handling a wave of migration that has been under way for several decades, as opposed to one that is just beginning. At the start, the host nation can look at the whole world, as America did in the 1960s, set broad limits, and wait to see who shows up. Three decades later, the gatekeepers must deal with a migration that has developed a momentum and a direction of its own.

...

... Setting new limits on immigration is not like setting a new national speed limit or a new set of minimum sentencing requirements for felonies. It is not simply a matter of picking a number and obliging everyone to live by it. Instead, it is more like setting interest rates or deciding emissions standards for industrial plants. Policymakers must deal with the expectations created by past decisions, as much as with the consequences of new ones....

A mature, well-developed migration of the sort that the United States is experiencing today does not lend itself to stroke-of-the-pen decisionmaking. It is impossible to start from scratch when confronting a demographic event that is three decades old and that involves nearly 20 million people in the United States and many millions more around the world. Rather than drastic or rapid changes, this is an area that demands decisions built upon past policies whenever possible. It is always politically tempting to declare a crisis and promote a sweeping solution. But immigration usually defeats such gambits, and as it gains momentum and matures it becomes even more resistant to one-shot solutions.

These seemingly familiar facts mask huge policy challenges. The size of the flow ensures that the immigration issue will be a matter of concern for years, probably for decades, to come. Immigrants and their children now account for half of the nation's population growth. Something so big doesn't go away quickly....

...

The fact that the immigrant population is intensely concentrated in a few areas of the country means that this issue is subject to considerable distortion both as a political and a practical matter.

Some 34 percent of the total foreign-born population lives in California—a concentration nearly four times greater than any other state, including the runner-up, Florida. This means that California, especially Southern California, has become an anomaly and is treated as such by policymakers. Like New York in the first half of this century, Southern California differs markedly in its basic character from any other place in the country because it hosts so many immigrants. This poses immediate and vexing challenges that will color the development of immigration policy in the short term. The first of these is: Who pays?

The costs of immigration are paid primarily at the local level. These include the added burdens on education and health systems, the administrative difficulties of dealing with a population of non-English speakers, and the economic dislocations that can be caused by a steady influx of new immigrant workers. Some of the benefits of immigration, such as the revival of deteriorating residential neighborhoods and the growth of small business, are enjoyed locally, but for the most part the benefits of immigration are derived primarily at the national level. These include a more mobile and flexible labor force, the constant augmentation of the talent pool with adults who were educated and trained elsewhere (and at someone else's expense), and the ability to use immigration as a foreign policy tool.

This imbalance between local costs and national benefits becomes especially acute when newly arrived immigrants cluster in a few places while they go through the most costly period of adaptation to American society, then move into other parts of the country (either later in life or when the second generation moves out) when their contributions are greater. This happened in the era of European immigration, and it appears to be happening again now.

...

Immigration is an area of policy that cries out for national consensus. Indeed, no broad direction can be set for immigration policy without some agreement on the national goals it seeks to accomplish. However, the high concentration of immigrants in just a few places creates distortions that make this kind of broad perspective much more difficult to reach.

Immigration politics and policy are further complicated by wide disparities in the economic and educational status of immigrants. The immigrant population includes both rich and poor, educated and illiterate. Compared to the average American, some immigrants are better off while others are worse off. As such, immigrants elicit both envy and disdain.

The remarkable polarization evident in the foreign-born population comes through most clearly in their levels of education upon arrival, as surveyed by the Census Bureau in 1994.

Recent adult immigrants—those who arrived since 1990 and are at least twenty-five years old—are more likely to have a college degree than native-born Americans by a large margin (21 percent, as compared to 15 percent). The gap is even wider as one moves higher up the educational ladder. While 11.5 percent of recent immigrants have graduate and professional degrees, only about 7.5 percent of native-born Americans have achieved that level of schooling. At the same time, a full 36 percent of the adult immigrant population has not graduated from high school, compared with only 17 percent of the native population.

...

While the foreign born do not mirror the U.S. population, neither do they reflect the world beyond America's borders. If immigrants were representative of the nations that sent them their qualifications would be even more heavily weighted toward the low end of the training scale. The United States is not simply replicating itself with foreign-born workers, nor is it being colonized by the Third World. Instead, immigration reflects the American future.

The educational characteristics of the foreign born are in demand in the newest and fastest-growing segments of the American labor market, such as high-tech manufacturing, finance, and services, all of which require workers with either exceptional training or little at all. America's rapidly evolving, postindustrial economy offers diminished opportunities and rewards for those in the middle, and it is in this vast center of the workforce where the greatest numbers of native-born workers compete for available jobs. Meanwhile, immigrants at either extreme find new jobs opening up for them.

Immigration has often satisfied the emerging demands of a changing economy. At the turn of the century, the European influx fed America's conversion to an urbanized and industrialized nation. But, especially at the beginning of that process—when America's character was still defined by small towns and rural life—few predicted that a blue-collar workforce made up of immigrants and their children would become a great engine of American strength and stability.

Now, as that industrial workforce and the economy it built fade from the scene, a new economy and a new workforce is emerging, and immigration is again contributing to the process. For policymakers this means that immigration becomes a part of the unpredictability and controversy that accompanies any broad process of economic and social change.

...

The connection with economic change is not always clear when immigrants begin filling a niche in the labor force, so it is difficult to predict the practical results of changes in immigration policy. But the challenges posed by the character of the immigrant flow go far beyond mere unpredictability.

...

Key Websites

ATLANTIC UNBOUND: IMMIGRATION

This website is an archive of articles originally published in *The Atlantic Monthly*. Some of the articles found here are: "Travels into America's Future" by Robert D. Kaplan (1998); "Should English Be the Law?" by Robert D. King (1997); "Can We Still Afford to Be a Nation of Immigrants?" by David M. Kennedy (1996); "The Coming Immigration Debate," by Jack Miles (1995); and "Must It Be the Rest against the West?" by Matthew Connelly and Paul Kennedy (1994). The website also provides factual data and links to other sites on the issue of immigration reform, and allows you to send e-mail to your senators and representatives.
http://www.theatlantic.com/unbound/flashbks/immigr/immigint.htm

CENTER FOR IMMIGRATION STUDIES

This website is the nation's only think tank devoted exclusively to research and policy analysis of the economic, social, demographic, fiscal, and environmental impact of immigration on the United States. The site includes links to other immigration-related sites.
http://www.us.net/cis/

UNITED STATES IMMIGRATION INFORMATION

This website includes a Fact Sheet on the Immigration Enforcement Improvements Act and other documents and press releases.
http://docs.whitehouse.gov/white-house-publications/1995/05/
   1995-05-03-fact-sheet-immigration-enforcement-improvements-
   act.text

THE FEDERATION FOR AMERICAN IMMIGRATION REFORM

The Federation for American Immigration Reform is an organization with 70,000 members who want to reform our nation's immigration laws. Their website contains publications, a history of immigration, polls, quizzes, a bulletin board, and related links.
http://www.fairus.org

IMMIGRATION CONTROL ASSOCIATION

The Immigration Control Association is a group of Californians working to stem the flow of immigrants into the United States. Their website includes numerous articles and links to organizations advocating limitation or moratorium on immigration.
http://www.immigrationmoratorium.com/

MIGRATION DIALOGUE

This website seeks to promote an informed discussion of the issues associated with international migration by providing unbiased and timely information on immigration and integration issues. The site includes newsletters, lists of experts on immigration and integration, essays, and links to related resources.
http://migration.ucdavis.edu

NATIONAL IMMIGRATION FORUM

The National Immigration Forum—a group dedicated to preserving America's tradition as a nation of immigrants—supports the reunification of families, the rescue and resettlement of refugees fleeing persecution, and the equal treatment of immigrants under the law. The group encourages immigrants to become U.S. citizens and promotes cooperation and understanding between immigrants and other Americans.
http://www.immigrationforum.org/

THE NATIONAL NETWORK FOR IMMIGRANT AND REFUGEE RIGHTS

The NNIRR serves as a forum to share information and analysis, to educate communities and the general public, and to develop and coordinate plans of action on important immigrant and refugee issues.
http://www.nnirr.org/

SUPREME COURT DECISIONS SEARCH

Immigration Online from Cornell University's Legal Information Institute.
http://www.law.cornell.edu/

HOOVER INSTITUTION ESSAYS ON PUBLIC POLICY

More than half of all immigrants to the United States reside in Los Angeles, New York, Chicago, Miami, San Diego, Houston, or San Francisco. An unresolved issue is whether immigrants are a benefit or a burden to these areas. A 1997 National Academy of Sciences study reports that "immigrants add as much as $10 billion to the national economy each year," but "in areas with high concentrations of low-skilled, low-paid immigrants," they impose net costs on U.S.-born workers. Stephen Moore, in "Immigration and the Rise and Decline of American Cities," questions that finding.
http://www-hoover.stanford.edu/publications/epp/epp81.html

Is the Discussion about Race and Intelligence Worthwhile?

In 1969 psychologist Arthur Jensen started a modern-day IQ debate, arguing that intelligence is a highly heritable trait, that differences in intelligence across races are quite possibly genetic, and that the high heritability of IQ could account for the failures of compensatory education programs.

Psychologist Richard Herrnstein (1971) added to the discussion by asserting that success in equalizing opportunity would make socioeconomic achievement increasingly dependent on genetic factors, and hence stratification would become increasingly rigid.

These themes were eventually brought together in the book *The Bell Curve*, a long and complex four-part book by Herrnstein and the political scientist Charles Murray. According to the authors, intelligence has a strong genetic component, plays a critical role in socioeconomic achievement and social pathology, and is becoming increasingly unequally distributed. This leads to an increasingly stratified society, a trend that they claim compensatory interventions cannot halt.

The Bell Curve noted that we are now approaching a world in which cognitive ability is the decisive dividing force.

Herrnstein and Murray believe IQ is at least 60 percent the result of heredity and about 40 percent due to the environment. They go on to assert the following:

> As a general rule, *as environments become more uniform, heritability rises*. When heritability rises, children resemble their parents more, and siblings increasingly resemble each other; in general, family members become more similar to each other and more different from people in other families. (p. 106)

Yet others argue that *The Bell Curve* pays too little attention to the environment. An environmental factor that Herrnstein and Murray ignore is the prevalence of females among blacks who score high on mental tests. Others who have done studies of high-IQ blacks have found several times as many females as males above the 120 IQ level. Since black males and black females have the same genetic inheritance, and if IQ differences of this magnitude can occur with no genetic difference at all, then it seems that some unusual environmental effects must be at work among blacks. However, these environmental effects need not be limited to blacks, for people of some other ancestries have likewise tended to have females over-represented among their higher scorers. One possible explanation is that females are more resistant to bad environmental conditions, as some other studies suggest.

Black males and black females are not the only groups to have significant IQ differences without any genetic differences. For example, identical twins with significantly different birthweights also have IQ differences, with the heavier twin averaging nearly 9 points higher IQ than the lighter one.

Charles Murray, in the article "The Bell Curve and Its Critics," defends *The Bell Curve* and argues that it is time to get serious about how best to accommodate the huge and often intractable individual differences that shape human society.

Even though he laments the limits facing low-IQ individuals in a postindustrial economy, he also claims to celebrate the capacity of people everywhere in the normal range on the bell curve to live morally autonomous, satisfying lives, if only the system will let them. Murray notes that accepting the message of *The Bell Curve* does not mean giving up on improving social policy; it means thinking anew about how progress is to be achieved—and even more fundamentally, thinking anew about how "progress" is to be defined.

Howard Gardner, in "Cracking Open the IQ Box," argues that the links between genetic inheritance and IQ, and then between IQ and social class, are much too weak to draw the inference that genes determine an individual's ultimate status in society. Nearly all of the reported correlations between measured intelligence and societal outcomes explain at most 20 percent of the variance. In other words, over 80 percent (and perhaps over 90 percent) of the factors contributing to socioeconomic status lie beyond measured intelligence. One's ultimate niche in society is overwhelmingly determined by non-IQ factors, ranging from initial social class to luck.

"The Bell Curve" and Its Critics

Charles
Murray

In November 1989, Richard Herrnstein and I agreed to collaborate on a book that, five years later, became *The Bell Curve*. It is a book about events at the two ends of the distribution of intelligence that are profoundly affecting American life. At one extreme, transformations in higher education, occupations, and federal power are creating a cognitive elite of growing wealth and influence. At the other extreme, transformations in occupations and social norms are creating a cognitive underclass. "Pressures from these contrasting movements at the opposite ends of society put terrific stress on the entire structure," we write in the preface, and we spend another 550 pages of main text and 300 pages of supplementary material explaining what we mean, and what we see as the implications for America's future.

It seems likely that *The Bell Curve* will be one of the most written-about and talked-about works of social science since the *Kinsey Report* 50 years ago. Most of the comment has been virulently hostile. The book is said to be the flimsiest kind of pseudo-science. Designed to promote a radical political agenda. A racist creed. Methodologically pathetic. Tainted by the work of neo-Nazis.

If any one generalization can be made about a work as long and diverse as *The Bell Curve*, it is that the book is relentlessly moderate—in its language, its claims, its science. It is filled with "on the one hand ... on the other hand" discussions of the evidence, presentations of competing explanations, cautions that certain issues are still under debate, and encouragement of other scholars to explore unanswered questions that go beyond the scope of our own work. The statistical analysis is standard and straightforward.

From *Commentary* 99, no. 5 (May 1995). Copyright © 1995. Reprinted with the permission of the author and *Commentary*.

Why then the hysteria? The obvious answer is race, the looming backdrop to all discussion of social policy in the United States. Ever since the first wave of attacks on the book, I have had an image of *The Bell Curve* as a sort of literary Rorschach test. I do not know how to explain the extraordinary discrepancy between what *The Bell Curve* actually says about race and what most commentators have said that the book says, except as the result of some sort of psychological projection onto our text.

Other factors are at work as well. Michael Novak (who has written favorably about *The Bell Curve*) and Thomas Sowell (who has his criticisms of the book) have pointed out in similar terms that the Left has invested everything in a few core beliefs about society as the cause of problems, government as the solution, and the manipulability of the environment for reaching the goal of equality. For the Left, as Novak puts it, *The Bell Curve*'s

> message cannot be true, because much more is at stake than a particular set of arguments from psychological science. A this-worldly eschatological hope is at stake. The sin attributed to Herrnstein and Murray is theological: They destroy hope.

The Bell Curve draws three important conclusions about intelligence and race: (1) All races are represented across the range of intelligence, from lowest to highest. (2) American blacks and whites continue to have different mean scores on mental tests, with the difference varying from test to test but usually about one standard deviation in magnitude—about fifteen IQ points. "One standard deviation" means roughly that the average black American scores at the sixteenth percentile of the white distribution. (3) Mental-test scores are generally as predictive of academic and job performance for blacks as for other ethnic groups. Insofar as the tests are biased at all, they tend to overpredict, not underpredict, black performance.

These facts are useful in the quest to understand why (for example) occupational and wage differences separate blacks and whites, or why aggressive affirmative action has produced academic apartheid in our universities. More generally, Herrnstein and I write that a broad range of American social issues cannot be interpreted without understanding the ways in which intelligence plays a role that is often, and wrongly, conflated with the role of race. When it comes to government policy, there was in our minds just one authentic implication: Return as quickly as possible to the cornerstone of the American ideal that people are to be treated as individuals, not as members of groups.

The furor over *The Bell Curve* and race has barely touched on these core points. Instead, the critics have been obsessed—no hyperbole here—with genes, trying to stamp out any consideration of the possibility that race differences have a genetic component.

For the record, what we said about genes, IQ, and race in the book is that a legitimate scientific debate is under way about the relationship of genes to race differences in intelligence; that it is scientifically prudent at this point to assume that both environment and genes are involved, in unknown proportions; and, most importantly, that people are getting far too excited about the whole issue. Genetically-caused differences are not as fearful, nor environmentally-caused differences as benign, as many think. What matters is not the source but the existence of group differences, and their intractability (for whatever reasons).

Six months into my post-*Bell Curve* life, I have concluded that Herrnstein and I were prematurely right on this point. Certainly we were right empirically when we observed that the public at large is fascinated by the possibility of genetic differences, and that the intellectual elites have been "almost hysterically in denial about that possibility," as we put it in the book.

Yet the critics, in insisting that the issue of genes really is a big deal, are once again going to produce the very effect they want to avert. In this instance, they have based their attacks on the premise that a full, fair look at the data will make the issue go away. None appears to have recognized that Herrnstein and I did not make nearly as aggressive a case for genetic differences as the evidence permits.

I still think Herrnstein and I were right, if prematurely: It is possible to live with the truth about genes and race, whatever it may be, without changing one's mind about how a liberal society should function. But whether we were right or wrong, the violent reaction is making sure that the full range of data will be brought to public attention.

Perhaps the most important section of *The Bell Curve* is Part II, "Cognitive Classes and Social Behavior." It describes the relationship of IQ to poverty, school-dropout rates, unemployment, divorce, illegitimacy, welfare, parenting, crime, and citizenship. To avoid the complications associated with race, it does all this for a sample of whites, using the National Longitudinal Study of Youth.

The eight chapters in Part II deal with questions like: "What role does IQ play in determining whether a woman has a baby out of wedlock?" Or: "What are the comparative roles of socioeconomic disadvantage and IQ in determining whether a youngster grows up to be poor as an adult?" These are fascinating questions. But you will have a hard time figuring out from the published commentary on *The Bell Curve* that such questions were even asked, let alone what the answers were.

Instead, the main line of attack has been that there is really no need to pay any attention to those chapters, because Herrnstein and Murray confuse correlation with causation; because IQ really does not explain much of the variance anyway; and because the authors' measure of socioeconomic background is in any case deficient. On all three counts, the critics are setting up a reexamination of the existing technical literature on social problems that will be intellectually embarrassing to them in the end.

Here is the truth: The relationships between IQ and social behaviors that we present in *The Bell Curve* are not only "significant" in the standard statistical sense of that phrase, they are powerful in a substantive sense, often much more powerful than the relationships linking social behaviors with the usual suspects (education, social status, affluence, ethnicity). In fact, Herrnstein and I actually understate the strength of the statistical record in *The Bell Curve*. The story is complex, but worth recounting because it tells so much about the academic response to *The Bell Curve*.

Raising the question of policy brings us to the last of my four examples of the potential backfire effect of attacks on *The Bell Curve*—the malleability of IQ. These attacks focused on Chapter 17, "Raising Cognitive Ability," which chronicles the record of attempts to raise IQ through better nutrition, prenatal care, infant intervention, and preschool and in-school programs. The cries of protest here have been almost as loud as those directed at our chapter on race, and for the reason that Michael Novak identified: By arguing that no easy methods for raising IQ exist, we "destroy hope," or at least the kind of hope that drives many of the educational and preschool interventions for today's disadvantaged youth.

We do express hope, actually. Because the environment plays a significant role (40 percent is our ball-park estimate) in determining intelligence— a point *The Bell Curve* states clearly and often—we say that sooner or later researchers ought to be able to figure out where the levers are. We urge that steps be taken to hasten the day when such knowledge becomes available.

But in examining the current state of knowledge, we also urge realism. Speaking of the most popular idea, intensive intervention for preschoolers, we conclude that "we and everyone else are far from knowing whether, let alone how, any of these projects have increased intelligence." We also predict that "many ostensibly successful projects will be cited as plain and indisputable evidence that we are willfully refusing to see the light."

A few weeks after *The Bell Curve* appeared, a reporter remarked to me that the real message of the book is "Get serious." I resisted at first, but I now think he had a point.

We never quite say it in so many words, but the book's subtext is that America's discussion of social policy since the 1960s has been carried on in a never-never land where human beings are easily changed and society can eventually become a Lake Wobegon where everyone is above average. *The Bell Curve* does indeed imply that it is time to get serious about how best to accommodate the huge and often intractable individual differences that shape human society.

This is a counsel not of despair but of realism—including realistic hope. An individual's "g" may not be as elastic as one would prefer, but the inventiveness of the species seems to have few bounds. In *The Bell Curve*, we are matter-of-fact about the limits facing low-IQ individuals in a postindustrial economy, but we also celebrate the capacity of people everywhere in the normal range on the bell curve to live morally autonomous, satisfying lives, if only the system will let them. Accepting the message of *The Bell Curve* does not mean giving up on improving social policy, it means thinking anew about how progress is to be achieved—and even more fundamentally, thinking anew about how "progress" is to be defined.

The verdict on the influence of *The Bell Curve* on policy is many years away. For now, the book may have another useful role to play that we did not anticipate. The attacks on it have often read like an unintentional confirmation of our view of the "cognitive elite" as a new caste, complete with high priests, dogmas, heresies, and apostates. They have revealed the extent to which the social science that deals in public policy has in the latter part of the 20th century become self-censored and riddled with taboos—in a word, corrupt. Only the most profound, anguished, and divisive reexamination can change that situation, and it has to be done within the profession. If *The Bell Curve* achieves nothing else, I will be satisfied if it helps get such a reexamination going.

Howard
Gardner

Cracking Open
the IQ Box

...

Taken at face value, *The Bell Curve* proceeds in straightforward fashion. Herrnstein and Murray summarize decades of work in psychometrics and policy studies and report the results of their own extensive analyses of the National Longitudinal Survey of Labor Market Experience of Youth, a survey that began in 1979 and has followed more than 12,000 Americans aged 14–22. They argue that studies of trends in American society have steadfastly ignored a smoking gun: the increasing influence of measured intelligence (IQ). As they see it, individuals have always differed in intelligence, at least partly because of heredity, but these differences have come to matter more because social status now depends more on individual achievement. The consequence of this trend is the bipolarization of the population, with high-IQ types achieving positions of power and prestige, low-IQ types being consigned to the ranks of the impoverished and the impotent. In the authors' view, the combined ranks of the poor, the criminal, the unemployed, the illegitimate (parents and offspring), and the uncivil harbor a preponderance of unintelligent individuals. Herrnstein and Murray are disturbed by these trends, particularly by the apparently increasing number of people who have babies but fail to become productive citizens. The authors foresee the emergence of a brutal society in which "the rich and the smart" (who are increasingly the same folks) band together to isolate and perhaps even reduce the ranks of those who besmirch the social fabric.

...

From *The American Prospect* 20 (winter 1995). Copyright © 1995 by New Prospect, Inc. Reprinted with the permission of The American Prospect, P.O. Box 383080, Cambridge, MA 02238.

Do Genes Explain Social Class?

In a textbook published in 1975, Herrnstein and his colleague Roger Brown argued that the measurement of intelligence has been the greatest achievement of twentieth-century scientific psychology. Psychometricians can make a numerical estimate of a person's intelligence that remains surprisingly stable after the age of five or so, and much convergent evidence suggests that the variations of this measure of intelligence in a population are determined significantly (at least 60 percent) by inheritable factors. As Herrnstein and Murray demonstrate at great length, measured intelligence correlates with success in school, ultimate job status, and the likelihood of becoming a member of the cognitively entitled establishment.

But correlation is not causation, and it is possible that staying in school causes IQ to go up (rather than vice versa) or that both IQ and schooling reflect some third causative factor, such as parental attention, nutrition, social class, or motivation. Indeed, nearly every one of Herrnstein and Murray's reported correlations can be challenged on such grounds. Yet, Herrnstein and Murray make a persuasive case that measured intelligence—or, more technically, "g," the central, general component of measured intelligence—does affect one's ultimate niche in society.

But the links between genetic inheritance and IQ, and then between IQ and social class, are much too weak to draw the inference that genes determine an individual's ultimate status in society. Nearly all of the reported correlations between measured intelligence and societal outcomes explain at most 20 percent of the variance. In other words, over 80 percent (and perhaps over 90 percent) of the factors contributing to socioeconomic status lie beyond measured intelligence. One's ultimate niche in society is overwhelmingly determined by non-IQ factors, ranging from initial social class to luck. And since close to half of one's IQ is due to factors unrelated to heredity, well over 90 percent of one's fate does not lie in one's genes. Inherited IQ is at most a paper airplane, not a smoking gun.

...

Psychology, Biology, and Culture

...

... A more empirically sensitive and scientifically compelling understanding of human intelligence has emerged in the past hundred years. Many authorities have challenged the notion of a single intelligence or even the concept of intelligence altogether. Let me mention just a few examples. (The works by Stephen Ceci and Robert Sternberg, as well as my own, discuss many more.)

Sternberg and his colleagues have studied valued kinds of intellect not measured by IQ tests, such as practical intelligence—the kind of skills and capacities valued in the workplace. They have shown that effective managers are able to pick up various tacit messages at the workplace and that this crucial practical sensitivity is largely unrelated to psychometric intelligence. Ralph Rosnow and his colleagues have developed measures of social or personal intelligence—the capacities to figure out how to operate in complex human situations—and have again demonstrated that these are unrelated to the linguistic and logical skills tapped in IQ tests.

Important new work has been carried out on the role of training in the attainment of expertise. Anders Ericsson and his colleagues have demonstrated that training, not inborn talent, accounts for much of experts' performances; the ultimate achievement of chess players or musicians depends (as your mother told you) on regular practice over many years. Ceci and others have documented the extremely high degree of expertise that can be achieved by randomly chosen individuals; for example, despite low measured intelligence, handicappers at the racetrack successfully employ astonishingly complex multiplicative models. A growing number of researchers have argued that, while IQ tests may provide a reasonable measure of certain linguistic and mathematical forms of thinking, other equally important kinds of intelligence, such as spatial, musical, or personal, are ignored (this is the subject of much of my own work). In short, the closed world of intelligence is being opened up.

Accompanying this rethinking of the concept of intelligence(s), there is growing skepticism that short paper-and-pencil tests can get at important mental capacities. Just as "performance examinations" are coming to replace multiple-choice tests in schools, many scientists, among them Lauren Resnick and Jean Lave, have probed the capacities of individuals to solve problems "on the scene" rather than in a testing room, with pencil and paper. Such studies regularly confirm that one can perform at an expert level in a natural or simulated setting (such as bargaining in a market or simulating the role of a city manager) even with a low IQ, while a high IQ cannot in itself substitute for training, expertise, motivation, and creativity. Rather than the pointless exercise of attempting to raise psychometric IQ (on which Herrnstein and Murray perseverate), this research challenges us to try to promote the actual behavior and skills that we want our future citizens to have. After all, if we found that better athletes happen to have larger shoe sizes, we would hardly try to enlarge the feet of the less athletic.

Scientific understanding of biological and cultural aspects of cognition also grows astonishingly with every passing decade. Virtually no serious natural scientist speaks about genes and environment any longer as if they were opposed. Indeed, every serious investigator accepts the importance of both biological and cultural factors and the need to understand their interactions. Genes regulate all human behavior, but no form of behavior will emerge without the appropriate environmental triggers or supports. Learning alters the way in which genes are expressed.

The development of the individual brain and mind begins in utero, and pivotal alterations in capacity and behavior come about as the result of innumerable events following conception. Hormonal effects in utero, which certainly are environmental, can cause a different profile of cognitive strengths and limitations to emerge. The loss of certain sensory capacities causes the redeployment of brain tissue to new functions; a rich environment engenders the growth of additional cortical connections as well as timely pruning of excess synapses. Compare a child who has a dozen healthy experiences each day in utero and after birth to another child who has a daily diet of a dozen injurious episodes. The cumulative advantage of a healthy prenatal environment and a stimulating postnatal environment is enormous. In the study of IQ, much has been made of studies of identical and fraternal twins. But because of the influences on cognition in utero and during infancy, even such studies cannot decisively distinguish genetic from environmental influences.

Herrnstein and Murray note that measured intelligence is only stable after age five, without drawing the obvious conclusion that the events of the first years of life, not some phlogiston-like "g," are the principal culprit. Scores of important and fascinating new findings emerge in neuroscience every year, but scarcely a word of any of this penetrates the Herrnstein and Murray black-box approach.

Precisely the same kind of story can be told from the cultural perspective. Cultural beliefs and practices affect the child at least from the moment of birth and perhaps sooner. Even the parents' expectations of their unborn child and their reactions to the discovery of the child's sex have an impact. The family, teachers, and other sources of influence in the culture signal what is important to the growing child, and these messages have both short- and long-term impact. How one thinks about oneself, one's prospects in this world and beyond, and whether one regards intelligence as inborn or acquired—all these shape patterns of activity, attention, and personal investments in learning and self-improvement. Particularly for stigmatized minorities, these signals can wreck any potential for cognitive growth and achievement.

Consider Claude Steele's research on the effects of stereotyping on performance. African-American students perform worse than white students when they are led to believe that the test is an intellectual one and that their race matters, but these differences wash out completely when such "stereotype vulnerable" conditions are removed.

To understand the effects of culture, no study is more seminal than Harold Stevenson and James Stigler's book *The Learning Gap: Why Our Schools Are Failing and What We Can Learn from Japanese and Chinese Education* (1992). In an analysis that runs completely counter to *The Bell Curve*, Stevenson and Stigler show why Chinese and Japanese students achieve so much more in schools than do Americans. They begin by demonstrating that initial differences in IQ among the three populations are either nonexistent or trivial. But with each passing year, East Asian students raise their edge over

Americans, so that by the middle school years, there is virtually no overlap in reading and mathematics performance between the two populations.

Genetics, heredity, and measured intelligence play no role here. East Asian students learn more and score better on just about every kind of measure because they attend school for more days, work harder in school and at home after school, and have better-prepared teachers and more deeply engaged parents who encourage and coach them each day and night. Put succinctly, Americans believe (like Herrnstein and Murray) that if they do not do well, it is because they lack talent or ability; Asians believe it is because they do not work hard enough. As a Japanese aphorism has it, "Fail with five hours of sleep; pass with four." Both predictions tend to be self-fulfilling. As educator Derek Bok once quipped, Americans score near to last on almost all measures save one: When you ask Americans how they think they are doing, they profess more satisfaction than any other group. Like Herrnstein and Murray, most Americans have not understood that what distinguishes the cultures is the pattern of self-understanding and motivation, especially the demands that we make on ourselves (and on those we care about) and the lessons we draw from success and failure—not the structure of genes or the shape of the brain.

...

Rhetorical Bomb-Throwing

Perhaps the most troubling aspect of the book is its rhetorical stance. This is one of the most stylistically divisive books that I have ever read. Despite occasional avowals of regret and the few utopian pages at the end, Herrnstein and Murray set up an us/them dichotomy that eventually culminates in an us-against-them opposition.

Who are "we"? Well, we are the people who went to Harvard (as the jacket credits both of the authors) or attended similar colleges and read books like this. We are the smart, the rich, the powerful, the worriers. And who are "they"? They are the pathetic others, those who could not get into good schools and who don't cut it on IQ tests and SATs. While perhaps perfectly nice people, they are simply not going to make it in tomorrow's complex society and will probably end up cordoned off from the rest of us under the tutelage of a vicious custodial state. The hope for a civil society depends on a miraculous return of the spirit of the Founding Fathers to recreate the villages of Thomas Jefferson or George Bailey (as played by Jimmy Stewart) or Beaver Cleaver (as played by Jerry Mather).

...

Why is this so singularly off-putting? I would have thought it unnecessary to say, but if people as psychometrically smart as Messrs. Herrnstein and Murray did not "get it," it is safer to be explicit. High IQ doesn't make a person one whit better than anybody else. And if we are to have any chance of a civil and humane society, we had better avoid the smug self-satisfaction of an elite that reeks of arrogance and condescension.

...

It is callous to write a work that casts earlier attempts to help the disadvantaged in the least-favorable light, strongly suggests that nothing positive can be done in the present climate, contributes to an us-against-them mentality, and then posits a miraculous cure. High intelligence and high creativity are desirable. But unless they are linked to some kind of a moral compass, their possessors might best be consigned to an island of glass-bead game players, with no access to the mainland.

KEY WEBSITES

INTELLIGENCE: KNOWNS AND UNKNOWNS

"Intelligence: Knowns and Unknowns," a report of a task force established by the Board of Scientific Affairs of the American Psychological Association: The first section of this report reviews the approaches to intelligence that are currently influential, or that seem to be becoming so. Much of the discussion is devoted to the dominant psychometric approach (IQ testing), which has inspired the most research and attracted the most attention. The views of several current theorists who argue that there are many different "intelligences," only a few of which can be captured by standard psychometric tests, are also presented.

· http://www.psych.nwu.edu/~eischens/know.html

CURVEBALL

Stephen Jay Gould, "Curveball," *New Yorker*, November 28, 1994: In this article, biologist Stephen Jay Gould argues that *The Bell Curve*, with its claims and supposed documentation that race and class differences are largely caused by genetic factors and are therefore essentially immutable, contains no new arguments and presents no compelling data to support its anachronistic social Darwinism. He concludes that its success in winning attention must reflect the depressing temper of our time when a mood for slashing social programs can be abetted by an argument that beneficiaries cannot be helped, owing to inborn cognitive limits expressed as low IQ scores.

http://www.dartmouth.edu/~chance/course/topics/curveball.html

IS INTELLIGENCE FIXED?

Nathan Glazer, "Is Intelligence Fixed?" *National Review* 46, no. 23 (December 5, 1994): 50(3): Glazer claims the authors of *The Bell Curve* make many valid points on differences in intelligence, but they fail to adequately explore the progress in narrowing the IQ gap between racial groups. Affirmative action is valid despite the conclusions of the book.

http://www.cycad.com/cgi-bin/Upstream/Issues/
    bell-curve/glazer.html

MAINSTREAM SCIENCE ON INTELLIGENCE

"Mainstream Science on Intelligence," *Wall Street Journal*, December 13, 1994: This statement signed by dozens of scientists outlines conclusions regarded as mainstream among researchers on intelligence, in particular, on the nature, origins, and practical consequences of individual and group differences in intelligence. Its aim is to promote more reasoned discussion of the vexing phenomenon that the research has revealed in recent decades.

http://www.cycad.com/cgi-bin/Upstream/Issues/bell-curve/
    support-bell-curve.html

RACE, GENES, AND IQ

Ned Block, "Race, Genes, and IQ," *Boston Review* 20, no. 6 (December/January 1995): 30–35: Block believes the Herrnstein/Murray argument on race and intelligence depends on conceptual confusions about the genetic determination of human behavior that have not been fully addressed.
http://www-polisci.mit.edu/BostonReview/BR20.6/block.html

REFLECTIONS ON MULTIPLE INTELLIGENCES: MYTHS AND MESSAGES

Howard Gardner, "Reflections on Multiple Intelligences: Myths and Messages": Gardner published "Frames of Mind: An Introduction to the Theory of Multiple Intelligences" (MI theory) in 1983. In this article, he discusses seven myths that have grown up about multiple intelligences and puts forth seven complementary "realities," with which he attempts to set the record straight.
http://www.byu.edu/~pe/pe658/reflections.HTML

AMERICA'S NEXT ACIIIEVEMENT TEST: CLOSING THE BLACK-WHITE TEST SCORE GAP

Christopher Jencks and Meredith Phillips, "America's Next Achievement Test: Closing the Black-White Test Score Gap," *The American Prospect*, no. 40 (September–October 1998): 44–53: The authors argue that the black-white test score gap does not appear to be an inevitable fact of nature. Despite endless speculation, no one has found genetic evidence indicating that blacks have less innate intellectual ability than whites. Thus while it is clear that eliminating the test score gap would require enormous effort by both blacks and whites and would probably take more than one generation, they believe it can be done.
http://epn.org/prospect/40/40jencfs.html

TWO VIEWS OF THE BELL CURVE

Two book reviews of Richard J. Herrnstein and Charles Murray, *The Bell Curve: Intelligence and Class Structure in American Life* (New York: Free Press, 1994), appeared in *Contemporary Psychology* 40, no. 5 (May 1995), the American Psychological Association's journal of book reviews: Reviews by Thomas J. Bouchard, Jr., "Breaking the Last Taboo," and Donald D. Dorfman, "Soft Science with a Neoconservative Agenda."
http://www.apa.org/journals/bell.html

Has Bilingual Education Been Abused?

For the past twenty years, bilingual education has been used to teach academic subjects to immigrant children in their native languages (most often Spanish), while slowly and simultaneously adding English instruction. In theory, the children don't fall behind in other subjects while they are learning English. When they are fluent in English, they can then "transition" to English instruction in academic subjects at the grade level of their peers. Further, the theory goes, teaching immigrants in their native language values their family and community culture and reinforces their sense of self-worth, thus making their academic success more likely.

Bilingual education's critics, however, tell a different story. In the early twentieth century, public schools assimilated immigrants to American culture and imparted workplace skills essential for upward mobility. Children were immersed in English instruction and, when forced to "sink or swim," they swam. Today, however, separatist (usually Hispanic) community leaders and their supporters, opposed to assimilation, want Spanish instruction to preserve native culture and traditions. This is problematic because the proximity of Mexico and the possibility of returning home give today's immigrants the option of "keeping a foot in both camps"—an option not available to previous immigrants who were forced to assimilate. According to the critics of bilingual education, today's attempts to preserve immigrants' native languages and cultures will not only balkanize the American melting pot but also hurt the children upon whom bilingual education is imposed because their failure to learn English well will leave them unprepared for the workplace. Bilingual education supporters may claim that it aims to teach English, but high dropout rates for immigrant children and low rates of transition to full English instruction show that, even if educators' intentions are genuine, the program is a failure.

In answer to these differing viewpoints, modern research findings on bilingual education are mixed. As with all educational research, it is so difficult to control for complex background factors affecting academic outcomes that no single study is ultimately satisfying.

In the article "Bilingual Education," Sheldon Richman contends that bilingual education is just one more of the faddish theories and politically motivated practices that teachers unions and departments of education have foisted on American children. The children are being used as guinea pigs for these ill-conceived theories that ultimately do more harm than good.

Barry McLaughlin, in "Myths and Misconceptions about Second Language Learning," attempts to clarify and dispel a number of myths that have evolved with respect to bilingual education. He believes that quick and easy solutions are not appropriate for an issue as complex as bilingual education. Second-language learning by school-aged children takes longer, is harder, and involves a great deal more than most people have been led to believe.

Bilingual Education
A Failed Experiment on the Children

Sheldon
Richman

...

Public schools in America have always been laboratories for social engineers. The children are the guinea pigs. The people in the schools of education, departments of educational psychology, the teachers unions, and the bureaucracy are the pseudoscientists who assure the parents of America that they know best while subjecting their children to faddish theories and politically motivated practices.

This was true from the very beginning. Horace Mann launched the "common school" movement with the promise that a national culture could be engineered by enlightened and well-meaning educational theorists who would put the nation's children through a scientifically conceived curriculum designed to create good citizens. The curriculum was in no sense scientifically designed; the mantle of science was used to hide a well-meaning but nevertheless politically motivated agenda. That approach to education necessarily interfered with the prerogatives of the family. In other words, bureaucrats made decisions that should have been made by parents.

The history of public, or state, schools has been a series of similar episodes. Terms such as "life adjustment," "new math," "whole language," "values clarification," and "family life" have become notorious shorthand for the social engineering approach of the schools. Should "bilingual education" be on that list? It seems so.

What Is Bilingual Education?

Bilingual education is one of several approaches to the teaching of what are called limited-English-proficient (LEP) children. Technically known as transitional bilingual education (TBE), this method is based on the theory that the best way to make minority-language children proficient in English is to first strengthen their skills in their native languages. In TBE, children learn to read and write in the native language, while theoretically getting an increasing amount of English instruction. The children are taught other subjects in the native language also. The ostensible purpose is to keep the children from falling behind in those subjects while they are learning English. It is important to understand that TBE is publicly defended as a way to ease the transition to English.

Christine Rossell of Boston University, who has studied bilingual education extensively, identifies three other basic approaches. Besides TBE, Rossell lists

- "submersion," in which no special assistance is provided to LEP children, who, like earlier generations of immigrants, take regular classes with English-speaking children;
- "English as a Second Language" (ESL), in which the children attend regular classes except for English instruction each day; and
- "structured immersion," in which the children learn all subjects in English but in a special class for LEP children where the teacher can take account of their English proficiency.

...

Who Are the Limited-English Proficient Children?

Much of the attention to limited-English proficiency goes to Spanish-speaking children. But of course there are many language minorities in the United States. According to the U.S. Department of Education, 73 percent of the roughly 3 million LEP students speak Spanish. The next biggest groups were Vietnamese (3.9 percent), American Indians (2.5 percent), Hmong (1.8 percent), Cantonese (1.7 percent), Cambodian (1.6 percent), and Korean (1.6 percent). Because of the relatively small number of non-Spanish-speaking LEP students and the difficulty in finding teachers fluent in the other languages, most of those students are instructed in English rather than their native languages.

...

Federal Involvement in Bilingual Education

Bilingual education grew out of the civil rights movement. Concern about racial minorities quickly extended to language minorities, particularly Hispanics, whose educational achievements were behind those of whites and blacks. That disparity was interpreted as a violation by the states and localities of the civil rights of Spanish-speaking people. Congress responded with two legislative acts:

- Title VI of the Civil Rights Act of 1964, which outlawed discrimination on the basis of race, color, or national origin in federally assisted programs, and
- The Bilingual Education Act of 1968 (Title VII of the Elementary and Secondary Education Act), which created the first federal bilingual education policy for language minority students and the mechanism for funding local school district programs.

As a result, the Office for Civil Rights (OCR) and the Office of Bilingual Education and Minority Languages Affairs (OBEMLA) were opened. Two bilingual education researchers, Christine H. Rossell and Keith Baker, point out that

> bilingual education became an organizing principle for politically active Hispanics who considered themselves uniquely excluded from the educational process by language and cultural problems not addressed in other programs. Bilingual advocates argued that the reason for Hispanic children on average having lower achievement than white children was the then-current practice of placing Spanish-speaking children in all-English regular classrooms and "forcing" them to give up their native tongue.

The early legislation did not specify any particular method of teaching; native-language was not mandated. The law merely authorized grants to local districts for research and experimental projects.

In 1974 the effort to involve the federal government in the issue of language minorities got a boost when the U.S. Supreme Court ruled in *Lau v. Nichols* that for limited-English-proficient children, identical education was not equal education. (The case was an interpretation of the Title VI of the Civil Rights Act.) The court said that a school district that accepts federal money must take "affirmative steps" to neutralize the language barriers of students whose native language is other than English. But the Court did not specify a remedy.

Nevertheless, *Lau* was critical in institutionalizing a systematic federal minority-language effort. The Office of Civil Rights set up a task force to propose policies to carry out the *Lau* principles. "The OCR task force recommendations, known as the '*Lau* remedies,' went well beyond the Court's requirement that school districts do something for LEP children," Rossell and Baker write. "The task force insisted that transitional bilingual education was the best, if not the only, instructional approach for providing equal educational opportunity to linguistic minorities." That policy direction was chosen without public discussion.

From 1975 to 1980 OCR contracted with 500 school districts to set up TBE programs. Districts that wished to use methods other than native-language instruction had to demonstrate the effectiveness of any alternative "even though OCR itself had never proven that TBE was effective." After *Lau*, Congress passed the Equal Educational Opportunities Act of 1974. In the same period, Congress amended Title VII to expand eligibility for the limited-English-proficiency children and to permit the enrollment of some English-speaking children. The amendments specified native-language instruction "to the extent necessary to allow a child to achieve competence in the English language." Thus, transitional bilingual education, as the name implies, was primarily construed as a means to turn limited-English-proficient children into fully English-proficient children. That fact will loom large when the results of TBE are contrasted with those of English-oriented programs.

...

The 1984 Bilingual Education Act gave states and local districts even greater leeway, permitting up to 4 percent of federal money (and in some cases 10 percent) to go to programs other than TBE. (Note the heavy tilt toward TBE despite the loosening of the rules.)

More flexibility was permitted in the 1988 reauthorization. Twenty-five percent of funds could go to English-language programs. "In addition, a three-year limit was placed on a student's participation in a transitional bilingual education program or in alternative instructional programs, although under special circumstances a student could continue in a program for up to two additional years."

The Elementary and Secondary Education Act was reauthorized in 1994, dubbed the Improving America's Schools Act. The reauthorized Title VII gave this ringing endorsement to TBE:

> the use of a child or youth's native language and culture in classroom instruction can ... promote self-esteem and contribute to academic achievement and learning English by limited English proficient children and youth. [§ 7102(a)14A.]

The Act also declared that "the Federal Government ... has a special and continuing obligation to ensure that States and local school districts take appropriate action to provide equal educational opportunities to children and youth of limited English proficiency." [§ 7102(a)15.]

When the goals of Title VII of the 1994 federal law were listed, the development of English proficiency was placed third, behind "developing systemic improvement and reform of educational programs serving limited English proficient students through the development and implementation of exemplary bilingual education programs and special alternative instruction programs" and "developing bilingual skills and multicultural understanding." [7102(b)(1) and (2)] When English proficiency is finally specified it is combined with "developing … the native language skills of such children and youth." [7102(b)(3)]

…

Thus, the weight of federal law is clearly behind native-language instruction, despite much rhetoric about local flexibility to encourage proficiency in English.

…

Considering the amount of money spent on and the passion behind the nearly 30-year-old bilingual movement, one would expect a volume of studies demonstrating the efficacy of the method. There appears to be no such documentation, however. Dispassionate researchers have concluded that, on the contrary, native-language instruction is an inferior method of moving limited-English-proficient children to full proficiency.

…

Porter argues that neither in theory nor in the data can one find support for the view that the best way to teach English to limited-proficient students is to spend several years teaching them their native languages (the so-called vernacular argument). "Nothing in my fifteen years in this field—from firsthand classroom experience to concentrated research—has begun to convince me that delaying instruction in English for several years will lead to better learning of English and to a greater ability to study subject matter taught in English," she writes. "When all the rhetoric is stripped away, the vernacular argument is still a hypothesis in search of legitimacy, and not a documented, empirically proven, successful method of second-language learning."

In her book, Porter reproduced a startling table drawn from the survey of research performed by Rossell and Baker. The table lists the percentage of "methodologically acceptable studies" that show the superiority, inferiority, or equality of transitional bilingual education, English as a Second Language, submersion (essentially doing nothing for LEP students), and structured immersion programs. The studies used reading, language, and math as indicators of the success of the methods. In no case did more studies show the superiority of TBE than showed its inferiority. A portion of the chart is reproduced below.

TBE versus Doing Nothing

	Reading	Language	Math
TBE Better	22%	7%	9%
No Difference	45%	29%	56%
TBE Worse	33%	64%	35%
# of studies	60	14	34

...

Among the studies worth noting is one conducted by the El Paso, Texas, Bilingual Immersion Project of 2,500 Spanish-speaking students from grade one to three. The students, all from similar economic backgrounds, were divided into native-language and English-immersion programs. The results were stark. Those in the immersion program performed better than those in TBE on standardized tests in reading and language. They did as well in math, and were above average in science and social studies.

Another indication of the inferiority of native-language instruction, according to researchers, is the exit rate from the various programs. The studies tend to show that students in English-oriented programs are "main-streamed" sooner than students in native-language programs. For example, a New York City Board of Education longitudinal study from 1990–94 found that of students who entered ESL programs in kindergarten, nearly 80 percent exited in three years, versus only 52 percent of students in bilingual classes. Of those who entered ESL in second grade, 68 percent left in three years, versus only 22 percent of those in bilingual programs.

In his introduction to the study, Chancellor Ramon C. Cortines wrote that it "showed that ESL-only students tested out of LEP services more quickly and that in the short term, those in ESL-only programs appeared to have better outcomes." Such results are reproduced in many places. Writes Porter:

> In both the El Paso and New York City longitudinal studies ... students in the English language, structured immersion programs met program goals in three to four years and were assigned to regular classrooms without special help, while students in the traditional bilingual classrooms needed six to seven years to reach the same level of mainstreaming.

Those studies undermine the theoretical claim that students will best learn English by first learning their native languages and then transferring those skills to English afterward. At least one advocate of bilingual education has trouble accepting that claim. The educational psychologist Kenji Hakuta has said, "What is remarkable about the issue of the transfer of skills is that despite its fundamental importance, almost no empirical studies have been conducted to understand the characteristics or even to demonstrate the existence of transfer of skills."

...

The Politics of Bilingual Education

If even prominent advocates of bilingual education acknowledge that solid evidence for its superiority is lacking, what gives the bilingual movement its potency? It is difficult to conclude other than that the push for bilingual education is bound up with an ideological agenda that has little to do with the education of children. Linda Chavez, president of the Center for Equal Opportunity, writes that from the start

> bilingual-education policy soon fell under the sway of political activists demanding recognition of the "group right" of cultural and linguistic minorities. By the late 1970s the federal civil-rights office was insisting that school districts offer bilingual education to Hispanic and other "language minority" students or face a cutoff of federal funds....

. . .

The American Institutes for Research evaluated federally supported bilingual programs and found, startlingly, that only 16 percent of students spoke only Spanish. Eighty-six percent of project directors said that when children became functional in English, they nevertheless stayed in the program.

. . .

The systematic placing of English-speaking students into Spanish-language programs smacks of a policy driven by ideology, not pedagogy. Chavez said bilingual education is part of an effort by Hispanic activists to establish Spanish as a "second national language." That term, in fact, was used by Josué González, director of bilingual education in the Carter Administration.

. . .

Conclusion

. . .

In many bilingual programs, Hispanic parents have no choice about whether their children will be educated in Spanish or English. Even where there is nominal choice, Roger Martinez says, parents are intimidated by the authority of the state's school system. This is wrong. Parents and children should be choosing educational objectives and buying the services that they believe will best achieve them. If parents want their children to have a bilingual education, they should be free to choose, and pay for, that. If they want monolingual instruction (in whatever language) that should be up to them. We know what the overwhelming majority of parents will choose. But that is not the point. The point is freedom.

. . .

Myths and Misconceptions about Second Language Learning
What Every Teacher Needs to Unlearn

Barry
McLaughlin

As more and more children enter schools from families in which English is not the language of the home, teachers face the daunting challenge of instructing children who have limited skills in the English language. It is becoming increasingly obvious that this experience is not limited to teachers in certain schools or certain parts of the country. All teachers need to know something about how children learn a second language. Intuitive assumptions are often mistaken, and children can be harmed if teachers have unrealistic expectations and an inaccurate understanding of the process of second language learning and its relationship to acquiring other academic skills and knowledge.

As any adult who has tried to learn another language can verify, second language acquisition can be a frustrating and difficult experience. This is no less the case for children, although there is a widespread belief that children are facile second language learners. This is one of a number of myths that this paper intends to debunk.

The purpose of this paper is to clarify a number of important issues in the area of second language learning by discussing commonly held myths or misconceptions.

Myth 1: Children Learn Second Languages Quickly and Easily

One frequently hears this proposition in various forms. It is asserted that children can learn languages faster than adults; that immigrant children translate for their parents who have not learned the language; and that child learners speak without a foreign accent, whereas this is impossible for adult learners.

Excerpt from *Myths and Misconceptions about Second Language: What Every Teacher Needs to Unlearn* (Washington, D.C.: Center for Applied Linguistics, 1992). Reprinted with the permission of the author.

Typically, when pressed, people asserting the superiority of child learners resort to some variant of the "critical period hypothesis." The argument is that children are superior to adults in learning second languages because their brains are more flexible (Lenneberg, 1967; Penfield & Roberts, 1959). They can learn languages easily because their cortex is more plastic than that of older learners. (The corollary hypothesis is the "frozen brain hypothesis," applied to adult learners.)

The critical period hypothesis has been questioned by many researchers in recent years and is presently quite controversial (Geneses, 1981; Harley, 1989; Newport, 1990). The evidence for the biological basis of the critical period has been challenged and the argument made that differences in the rate of second language acquisition may reflect psychological and social factors, rather than biological ones that favor child learners. For example, children may be more motivated than adults to learn the second language. There is probably more incentive for the child on the playground and in school to communicate in the second language than there is for the adult on the job (where they often can get by with routine phrases and expressions) or with friends (who may speak the individual's first language anyway). It frequently happens that children are placed in more situations where they are forced to speak the second language than are adults.

. . .

Nonetheless, people continue to believe that children learn languages faster than adults. Is this superiority illusory? One difficulty in answering this question is that of applying the same criteria of language proficiency to both the child and the adult. The requirements to communicate as a child are quite different from the requirements to communicate as an adult. The child's constructions are shorter and simpler, and vocabulary is relatively small when compared with what is necessary for adults to speak at the same level of competence in a second language as they do in their first language. The child does not have to learn as much as an adult to achieve competence in communicating. Hence there is the illusion that the child learns more quickly than the adult, whereas when controlled research is conducted, in both formal and informal learning situations, results typically indicate that adult (and adolescent) learners perform better than young children.

What Does This Mean for the Teacher?

One of the implications of this line of research is that teachers should not expect miraculous results from children who are learning English as a second language (ESL) in the classroom context. At the very least, they should expect that learning a second language is as difficult for a child in their class as it is for the teachers as adults. In fact, it may be more difficult, as young children do not have access to the memory techniques and other strategies that more experienced learners can use in acquiring vocabulary and in learning the grammatical rules of the language.

...

Myth 2: The Younger the Child, the More Skilled in Acquiring a Second Language

A related myth concerns the best time to start language instruction. Certainly the optimal way to learn a second language is to begin at birth and learn two languages simultaneously. However, when should a young child who has acquired a first language begin a second? Some researchers take a younger-is-better position and argue that the earlier children begin to learn a second language, the better (e.g., Krashen, Long, & Scarcella, 1979). However, at least with regard to school settings, the research literature does not support this conclusion.

For example, a study of 17,000 British children learning French in a school context indicated that, after five years of exposure, children who had begun French instruction at age eleven performed better on tests of second language proficiency than children who had begun at eight years of age (Stern, Burstall, & Harley, 1975). The investigators in this study, the largest single study of children learning a second language in a formal classroom setting, concluded that older children are better second language learners than are younger ones.

...

Pronunciation is one aspect of language learning where the younger-is-better hypothesis may have validity. A number of studies have found that the younger one begins to learn a second language, the more native-like the accent one develops in that language (Asher & Garcia, 1969; Oyama, 1976). This may be because pronunciation involves motor patterns that have been fossilized in the first language and are difficult to alter after a certain age because of the nature of the neurophysiological mechanisms involved. It may also be that we do not understand very well how to teach phonology in a second language. Perhaps if we could develop more advanced (e.g., computer-assisted) methods of instruction, older learners might do better at acquiring a native-like accent in the second language.

Aside from the question of pronunciation, however, the younger-is-better hypothesis does not have strong empirical support in school contexts. The research suggests that younger children do not necessarily have an advantage over older children and, because of their cognitive and experiential limitations when compared to older children, are actually at a disadvantage in how quickly they learn a second language—other things being equal.

What Does This Mean for the Teacher?

The research cited above does not mean that early exposure to a second language is in some way detrimental to a child. An early start for foreign language learners, for example, allows for a long sequence of instruction leading to potential communicative proficiency. It also allows children to view second language learning and the insights they acquire into another culture as normal and integral parts of schooling. However, instruction of children with limited English proficiency in the United States involves different considerations from foreign language instruction in the United States or Europe or from French immersion in Canada. Language minority children in American schools need to master English as quickly as possible while at the same time learning subject-matter content. This suggests that in the American context early exposure to English is called for. However, because second language acquisition takes time, children will continue to need the support of their first language, where this is possible, so as not to fall behind in content-area learning.

...

Myth 3: The More Time Students Spend in a Second Language Context, the Quicker They Learn the Language

For many educators, the most straightforward way for children from non-English-speaking backgrounds to learn English is for them to be in an environment where they are constantly exposed to English. This is the rationale behind what is called "structured immersion," an instructional strategy in which children from language minority backgrounds receive all of their instruction in English and have the additional support of ESL classes and content-based instruction that is tailored to their language abilities.

Such a program has the advantage of providing more time on task for learning English than in a bilingual classroom. On the face of it, one might expect that the more English children hear and use, the quicker their English language skills develop. However, research evidence indicates that this is not necessarily the case. Over the length of the program, children in bilingual classes, where there is exposure to the home language and to English, have been found to acquire English language skills equivalent to those acquired by children who have been in English-only programs (Cummins, 1981; Ramirez, Yuen, & Ramey, 1991). This would not be expected if time on task were the most important factor in language learning.

Furthermore, many researchers caution against withdrawing the support of the home language too soon. There is a great deal of evidence that, whereas oral communication skills in a second language may be acquired within two or three years, it may take up to four to six years to acquire the level of proficiency for understanding the language in its instructional uses (Collier, 1989; Cummins, 1981). This is a point I shall return to in the next myth.

What Does This Mean for the Teacher?

Teachers should be aware that giving language minority children the support of their home language, where this is possible, is not doing them a disservice. The use of the home language in bilingual classrooms enables the child to avoid falling behind in school work, and it also provides a mutually reinforcing bond between the home and the school. In fact, the home language acts as a bridge for children, enabling them to participate more effectively in school activities while they are learning English.

The research indicates that, over the long run, children in bilingual programs will acquire as much English as children who have more exposure from an earlier age. Furthermore, if the child is able to acquire literacy skills in the first language, as an adult he or she may be functionally bilingual, with a unique advantage in technical or professional careers.

...

Myth 4: Children Have Acquired a Second Language Once They Can Speak It

Often, teachers assume that once children can converse comfortably in English, they are in full control of the language. Yet for school-aged children, there is much more involved in learning a second language than learning how to speak it. A child who is proficient in face-to-face communication has not necessarily achieved proficiency in the more abstract and disembedded academic language needed to engage in many classroom activities, especially in the later grades. For example, the child needs to learn what nouns and verbs are and what synonyms and antonyms are. Such activities require the child to separate language from the context of actual experience and to learn to deal with abstract meanings.

...

What Does This Mean for the Teacher?

...

Aside from this question, all teachers in all programs need to be aware that a child who is learning in a second language may be having language problems in reading and writing that are not apparent if the child's oral abilities are used as the gauge of English proficiency. It is conceivable that many of the problems that children from minority language backgrounds have in reading and writing at the middle school and high school levels stem from limitations in vocabulary and syntactic knowledge in the second language. Even children who are skilled orally can have these gaps. As we have seen, learning a second language is not an easy enterprise and is not finished in a year or two.

Myth 5: All Children Learn a Second Language in the Same Way

Most likely, if asked, teachers would not admit that they think all children learn a second language in the same way or at the same rate. Yet this seems to be the assumption underlying a great deal of practice. There are two

issues here: The first relates to differences among linguistically and culturally diverse groups and the second to differences among learners within
these groups.

Research indicates that mainstream American families and the families
of many children from minority cultural backgrounds have different ways
of talking (Heath, 1983; Ochs, 1982). Mainstream children are accustomed
to an analytic style, in which the truth of specific arguments is deduced from
general propositions. Many children from culturally diverse groups are
accustomed to an inductive style of talking, in which fundamental assumptions must be inferred from a series of concrete statements.

Schools in America emphasize the language functions and styles of
talk that predominate in mainstream families. Language is used to communicate meaning, to convey information, to control social behavior, and to
solve problems. In the upper grades, especially, the style of talk is analytic
and deductive. Children are rewarded for clear and logical thinking. It is no
wonder that children who come to school accustomed to using language in
a manner that is very different from what is expected in school experience
tension and frustration.

Furthermore, there are social class differences. In urban centers of literate, technologically advanced societies, middle-class parents teach their
children through language. Instructions are given verbally from a very early
age. This contrasts to the experience of immigrant children from less technologically advanced non-urbanized societies. Traditionally, teaching in
such cultures is carried out primarily through nonverbal means (Rogoff,
1990). Technical skills, such as cooking, driving a car, or building a house,
are learned through observation, supervised participation, and self-initiated
repetition. There is none of the information testing through questions that
characterizes the teaching-learning process in urban and suburban middle-
class homes.

In addition, some children in some cultures are more accustomed to
learning from peers than from adults. From their earliest years, they were
cared for and taught by older siblings or cousins. They learned to be quiet
in the presence of adults and had little experience in interacting with them.
When they enter school, they are more likely to pay attention to what their
peers are doing than to what the teacher is saying. At this point, the other
children are more important to them than adults.

...

What Does This Mean for the Teacher?

Teachers need to be aware of cultural and individual differences in learner
styles. Many culturally and linguistically diverse children enter school with
cognitive and social norms that differ from those that govern the mainstream classroom. These differences, in turn, affect the teacher's expectations of the child's ability and the teacher's response to the child. Within

the school environment, behaviors such as paying attention and persisting at tasks are valued. Because of their cultural background, however, some children may be less able to make the functional adaptation to the interpersonal setting of the school culture. Unless the teacher is aware of such cultural differences, the child's lack of attentiveness and lack of persistence can influence the teacher's expectations and the way the teacher interacts with these children.

...

Where Do We Go from Here?

Research on second language learning has shown that there are many misconceptions about how children learn languages. Teachers need to be aware of these research findings and to unlearn old ways of thinking. For the most part, this means realizing that quick and easy solutions are not appropriate for complex problems. Second language learning by school-aged children takes longer, is harder, and involves a great deal more than most teachers have been led to believe. We need consciously to rethink what our expectations should be.

Too often one hears of the "problem" of cultural and linguistic diversity in our country's schools, rather than the "opportunity" that diversity provides. Children from diverse backgrounds enrich our schools and our other students. Student diversity challenges the educational system, but the educational innovations and instructional strategies that are effective with diverse students can benefit all students.

KEY WEBSITES

NCBE (NATIONAL CLEARINGHOUSE FOR BILINGUAL EDUCATION) ROUNDTABLE ELECTRONIC DISCUSSION GROUP

NCBE is a very active Internet mailing list that focuses on bilingual education and other issues affecting linguistically and culturally diverse students. If you have specific problems and/or questions you would like to address, this discussion list offers a way to obtain advice from experts in the field of multilingual/multicultural education.

http://www.ncbe.gwu.edu/majordomo/

CENTER FOR MULTILINGUAL, MULTICULTURAL RESEARCH

The Center is an organized research unit at the University of Southern California, facilitating the research, collaboration, dissemination, and professional development activities of faculty, students, and others. The Center provides a base for those interested in multilingual education, English-as-a-second-language, foreign language instruction, multicultural education and related areas, and the opportunity to come together for research and program collaboration. There are four principal activities the Center focuses on: (1) research; (2) publications; (3) training; and (4) public service.

http://lmrinet.gse.ucsb.edu/

NATIONAL CLEARINGHOUSE FOR BILINGUAL EDUCATION

This site is by far the most comprehensive and informative site on Bilingual Education on the Internet. The National Clearinghouse for Bilingual Education (NCBE) is funded by the U.S. Department of Education's Office of Bilingual Education and Minority Languages Affairs (OBEMLA) to collect, analyze, and disseminate information relating to the effective education of linguistically and culturally diverse students in the United States.

http://www.ncbe.gwu.edu/

OFFICE OF BILINGUAL EDUCATION AND MINORITY LANGUAGE AFFAIRS

OBEMLA was established in 1974 by Congress to help school districts provide equal education opportunity to limited English proficient children.

http://www.ed.gov/offices/OBEMLA/

BILINGUAL EDUCATION NETWORK (BIEN)

The Bilingual Education Network is maintained by the California Department of Education and provides information relating to bilingual education.

http://www.cde.ca.gov/cilbranch/bien/bien.htm

UNIVERSITY OF CALIFORNIA LINGUISTIC MINORITY RESEARCH INSTITUTE (LMRI)

The University of California Linguistic Minority Research Institute (LMRI) provides information on issues of language, education, and public policy as they relate to linguistic minorities.

http://lmrinet.gsc.ucsb.edu/

Is Transracial Adoption Cultural Genocide?

Issues that involve children or race often inspire intense interest and emotion. Transracial adoption touches on both of these. It also raises several other issues. How much power should the state have to affect individual choices with respect to family life? How much assistance should the state provide to families in trouble before removing children from their parents? Most importantly, the subject of transracial adoption forces us to think about race not as a workplace or social contact issue, but in that more intimate context of the family.

To some people, transracial adoption is a harbinger of hope: If the different races can live together and love each other as members of the same family, surely there must be hope for the relationship between the races in the larger society.

African-American children are over-represented in the foster care population as a whole, and are only half as likely to be adopted as white children. This issue raises serious policy and practice questions about the most effective strategies to serve children of color.

In response to these concerns, federal law was recently changed to attempt to facilitate the transracial adoption of these children. Underlying this new legislation was the belief that children of color, in general, and African-American children, in particular, are not being adopted because of race-based decision making in adoptive placements. The expectation underlying this policy is that eliminating race as a consideration in adoptive placements will facilitate the adoption of children of color by white families, resulting in a large pool of white families coming forward to adopt these children.

This position has largely been supported by anecdotal accounts and by some data that white families have sought and been deprived of the opportunity to adopt African-American children and other children of color. Other families have sought alternate forms of adoption, such as international adoption, because of rejection by the child welfare system.

Those who oppose the facilitation of transracial adoption contend that there are prospective African-American families and other adoptive families of color, but barriers within the child welfare system historically have made it difficult for these families to adopt children in foster care.

Leora Neal, in "The Case against Transracial Adoption," agrees with a 1994 position paper from the National Association of Black Social Workers. This paper states the organization's current policy regarding transracial adoptions: (1) All efforts should be made to keep children with their biological relatives via preventive services or to return those children who are already in foster care; (2) for those children who cannot return to relatives, adoption by a family of the same race and culture is the next best option to preserve cultural continuity; and (3) transracial adoptions should be a last resort only after a documented failure to find an African-American home. Transracial placements should be reviewed and supported by representatives of the African-American community.

Randall Kennedy, in "Orphans of Separatism," points out that while one reason for favoring same-race placements of black children is that African-American parents can better equip African-American children with what they will need to know in order to survive and prosper in a white-dominated society, a counterview has just as much plausibility: namely, that white adults, as insiders to the dominant racial group in America, will know more than racial minorities about the inner world of whites and how best to maneuver with and around them in order to advance one's interests in a white-dominated society.

Other proponents of racial matching imply that white foster or adoptive parents will be, on average, less capable of instilling within a black child an appropriate sense of self-worth and an appropriate racial identity. But Kennedy notes that "there exists ... no consensus on how best to raise a black child (or, for that matter, any other sort of child) or on what constitutes a proper sense of self worth or on what constitutes an appropriate racial identity or on how one would go about measuring any of these things."

Kennedy also points out that another reason for racial matching in adoption is the belief that it may serve to save a child from placement in a family setting in which the child will be made to feel uncomfortable by a disapproving surrounding community. Yet this sounds like a regrettable concession to allow bigotry to shape adoption practices. In the past, one of the justifications for segregation was that it protected blacks from the wrath of those whites who would strongly object to the integration of public schools or accommodations in hotels and restaurants.

Kennedy believes that racial matching is a disastrous social policy both in how it affects children and in what it signals about our current attitudes regarding racial distinctions. In terms of immediate consequences, strong forms of racial matching block some parentless children from access to adults who would otherwise be deemed suitable as parents except that they are disqualified on the grounds that they are of the "wrong" race.

Kennedy notes that racial matching has diffuse, long-term moral and political consequences. It reinforces racialism. It strengthens the notion that race is destiny. It buttresses the notion that people of different racial backgrounds really are different in some moral, unbridgeable, permanent sense. Kennedy points out that racial matching affirms the notion that race should be a cage to which people are assigned at birth and from which people should not be allowed to wander.

The Case against Transracial Adoption

Leora
Neal

The National Association of Black Social Workers is an international organization composed of social workers and others in related fields. The purpose of the organization is to address itself to social welfare issues affecting Black peoples no matter where they happen to reside in the world and to bring services to African-American communities.

In 1972, at its fourth annual conference, held in Memphis, Tennessee, the National Association of Black Social Workers (NABSW) issued a resolution opposing the growing practice of placing African-American children in need of adoptive homes with Caucasian parents. The resolution was not based on racial hatred or bigotry, nor was it an attack on White parents. The resolution was not based on any belief that White families could not love Black children, nor did we want African-American children to languish in foster care rather than be placed in White adoptive homes.

Our resolution, and the position paper that followed, was directed at the child welfare system that has systematically separated Black children from their birth families. Child welfare workers have historically undertaken little effort to rehabilitate African-American parents, to work with extended families, or to reunite children in foster care with their families. Further, Black families and other families of color who tried to adopt waiting children were often met with discrimination or discouragement.

Accordingly, the NABSW took a position against transracial adoption in order to: (1) preserve African-American families and culture; (2) enable African-American children to appreciate their culture of origin through living within a family of the same race and culture; (3) enable African-

From *Focal Point* 10, no.1 (spring 1996). Copyright © 1996 by the Regional Research Institute for Human Services. Reprinted with the permission of the publishers and author.

American children to learn how to cope with racism through living with families who experience racism daily and have learned to function well in spite of that racism; and (4) break down the systemic barriers that make it difficult for African-American and other families of color to adopt.

This position forced child care agencies to examine their policies and helped to highlight the inequities in the child welfare system that did not give African-Americans equal access to African-American children (Neal & Stumph, 1993). It also made agencies take into consideration the concept of the importance of maintaining the child's culture and heritage of origin. However, they did not always take the next step in consistently accessing the African-American community in order to recruit Black families. Further, African-American families are often discouraged, discriminated against, or "screened out" of the adoption process because of cultural misunderstandings, racist attitudes, and ethnocentrism on the part of staff, as well as economic factors (such as high fees, low income). Studies such as *Barriers to Same Race Placement* (1991) conducted by the North American Council on Adoptable Children and Festinger's 1972 study *Why Some Choose Not to Adopt through Agencies* attest to these facts. The 1986 Westat Incorporated *Adoptive Services for Waiting Minority and Non-Minority Children* study showed that when the Black community perceived that a child caring agency was welcoming toward African-Americans, the agency had no problem making adoptive placements within the community. On the other hand, if the community perceived a child caring agency as not being "user friendly" they would not patronize the agency.

Barriers to Same Race Placement also revealed that agencies run by African-Americans were successful in placing 94 percent of their Black child population with African-American families. Child caring agencies who are having difficulty working with the African-American community need to consult with Black-run agencies to learn their successful strategies. Among others, the success of the Association of Black Social Workers' Child Adoption, Counseling and Referral Service (New York Chapter), Homes for Black Children (Detroit), the Institute for Black Parents (Los Angeles), Roots, Inc. (Georgia), and the One Church One Child Program (nationwide), have dispelled the myth that Black families do not adopt.

Adoption has always been part of the culture of Black people in Africa, the United States and in the Caribbean. Transracial placements are simply not necessary for the majority of Black children available for adoption. Hill's study *Informal Adoptions among Black Families* (1977) revealed that 90 percent of African-American children born out of wedlock are informally adopted. Gershenson's study *Community Response to Children Free for Adoption* (published by the U.S. Department of Health and Human Services, 1984) demonstrates that—with respect to formal adoptions through child caring agencies and the courts—African-American families adopt at a rate 4.5 times greater than any other ethnic group. If the barriers that keep thousands of African-Americans from adopting were eliminated and recruitment efforts were consistent and ongoing, Black children would be placed in African-American homes in even greater numbers.

Hill's *Black Pulse Survey*, conducted in 1981 and 1993, showed that there were three million African-American households interested in adoption. There are approximately 69,000 children with the goal of adoption nationwide and 43 percent of these children are African-American (U.S. Department of Health and Human Services, 1990). If only a fraction of the families interested in adoption were approved there would be enough African-American families to adopt Black children.

Children remain in foster care rather than being returned to relatives or adopted in an expeditious manner because there is a financial disincentive to release large numbers of children. Public and some private agencies receive governmental funds of $15,000 to $100,000 per year per child. These funds, tied to the numbers of children in foster care, are used to keep the agencies in business. If large numbers of children were released at any given time and were not replaced by equal numbers of children, an agency would have to downsize or close down. Foster care has become a billion dollar industry! Private agencies that receive no governmental monies often charge high fees. Beside the fact that fees of $2,000 to $9,000 per child create a financial hardship for some families, many Black families feel that paying fees is akin to slavery (buying children) and are angered by the practice. Therefore, one-half of the Black children placed by private agencies who do not receive governmental purchase of service fees are adopted transracially (Gilles & Kroll, 1991).

Transracial adoptions have increased due to the shortage of White infants and toddlers available for adoption. Contrary to the popular myth, transracial adoptions will have little effect in decreasing the large numbers of children in foster care because most of the children are school-aged or are children with special needs. Only four percent of children available for adoption nationwide are infants and toddlers under the age of two (U.S. Department of Health and Human Services, 1990). However, the majority of White families who would consider a transracial adoption want infants and toddlers. There is no shortage of Black families for such children.

It should be noted that 44 percent of the children available for adoption nationwide are White (mostly school-age and/or have special needs). However, there is little discussion concerning these children and their right to a permanent home. There is no suggestion from proponents of transracial adoptions that White children who are "languishing in the system" be adopted by African-Americans or other people of color. African-American families who have tried to adopt White children have been blocked by child caring agencies and the courts most of the time. Accordingly, in practice, transracial adoptions are a "one-way street." The question arises whether the thrust for increasing transracial adoptions is truly concerned with the "best interests of Black children" or "the right of [W]hite people to parent whichever child they choose?" (Perry, 1993–94).

Adoption is supposed to be a service to children, not parents. Adult adoptees of all races state that they have a human right to know their heritages. They are demanding more openness in adoptions and are searching for their biological relatives. Children placed with families of the same culture and race suffer great loss issues due to their separation from their biological families. Children placed transracially suffer a double loss because they have lost their cultural and racial connections as well (Verrier, 1993).

Many adult transracial adoptees report that, once they leave home, they feel that they do not belong anywhere. On the one hand they are not fully accepted in the White community and—even though they are more accepted in the Black community—they often do not understand various cultural nuances. Race and culture cannot be ignored. "The key to successful living as a minority person in a discriminating, denigrating society is to have positive affirmation with others like oneself, from whom one can gain support and affirmation and learn coping skills" (Howe, 1995).

The National Association of Black Social Workers has first and foremost been concerned with the preservation of African-American families. Very little effort has been put forth by the child welfare system to keep families together or to return children in foster care to their relatives. It is much more economical to keep children in their families than it is to fund their foster care. Unfortunately, preventive service programs are in danger of being cut by federal, state and local governments. Children come into foster care because of poverty-related issues. To deny help to these families is to ignore their strengths and to deny the importance of strengthening African-American communities to support the positive functioning of Black children.

Therefore, in 1994 the NABSW issued a paper on preserving African-American families. This paper states the organization's current policy regarding transracial adoptions: (1) All efforts should be made to keep children with their biological relatives via preventive services or return those children who are already in foster care; (2) For those children who cannot return to relatives, adoption by a family of the same race and culture is the next best option to preserve cultural continuity; and (3) Transracial adoptions should be a last resort only after a documented failure to find an African-American home. Transracial placements should be reviewed and supported by representatives of the African-American community (NABSW, 1994).

For those children who must be placed transracially, it must be remembered that White adoptive families become "mixed" families after they adopt transracially. They have to be given pre- and post-adoption services to enable them to help their children cope with racism and culture of origin disconnection. Many transracial adoptees bemoan the fact that their adoptive parents were ill-equipped to help them with these issues and that their self-esteem suffered as a result. The child welfare system must become more culturally competent and recognize that infants as well as older children grieve over their biological family and cultural losses.

The NABSW launched its Fist Full of Families Nationwide Adoption Initiative during the October 1995 Million Man March in Washington, D.C. and has received over 9,000 adoption inquiries in the subsequent six months. The expression of such a volume of interest in adoption demonstrates that, for the majority of African-American children, transracial adoptions are unnecessary.

Orphans of Separatism
The Painful Politics
of Transracial Adoption

Randall
Kennedy

No issue more highlights feelings of ambivalence over the proper place of racial distinctions in American life than the delicate matter of transracial adoptions. Opponents of such adoptions insist that allowing white adults to raise black children is at worst tantamount to cultural genocide and at best a naive experiment doomed to failure....

...

... [I]ncreasingly large numbers of children bereft of functioning parents are flooding social welfare agencies. Agencies are charged with maintaining these young refugees from destroyed families and either placing them in the temporary care of foster parents or the permanent care of adoptive parents.

Like most social catastrophes in the United States, this one weighs most heavily upon racial minority communities: The percentage of minority children in need of foster care or adoptive homes is far greater than their percentage of the population. In Massachusetts, approximately 5 percent of the population is black, yet black children constitute nearly half of the children in need of foster care or adoptive homes. In New York City, 75 percent of the nearly 18,000 children awaiting adoption are black. Nationwide, there are about 100,000 children eligible for adoption; 40 percent are black. While two years and eight months is the median length of time that children in general wait to be adopted, the wait for black children is often twice that long.

Conceiving of the deprivations suffered by children without parents is both easy and difficult. It is easy because some of the things that we expect

From *The American Prospect* 17 (spring 1994). Copyright © 1994 by New Prospect, Inc. Reprinted with the permission of The American Prospect, P.O. Box 383080, Cambridge, MA 02238.

parents to do are so obviously important. We expect parents to protect the interests of their children in a singular fashion, to show a degree of loyalty that cannot be bought, to demonstrate a mysterious allegiance deeper than professional duty. It is difficult because of the enormity of even attempting to calibrate the manifold, subtle, perhaps even unknowable losses borne by parentless children. There is one thing, however, about which we can be sure: It is a tragic condition indeed for a child to be condemned to the limbo of parentlessness, to suffer the loneliness of having no one to call "mother" or "father," to be exposed to the anxiety of having no family that is permanently and intimately one's own.

A second social disaster compounds the first. It is the disaster of racial matching itself. Racial-matching policies can vary in intensity, from absolute prohibitions against transracial child placements to temporary preferences for same-race placements. Examples of the former are state laws in the segregationist Jim Crow South that forbade adoption across the race line and, more recently, the position of the National Association of Black Social Workers, which categorically opposes transracial adoptions involving black children and white parents....

Racial matching is a disastrous social policy both in how it affects children and in what it signals about our current attitudes regarding racial distinctions. In terms of immediate consequences, strong forms of racial matching block some parentless children from access to adults who would otherwise be deemed suitable as parents except that they are disqualified on the grounds that they are of the "wrong" race. In some jurisdictions, the relevant decision-makers simply refuse to permit child placements across the color line. In others, authorities will permit foster care across racial lines but then remove the child if they move to deepen the relationship from mere temporary foster care to permanent adoption. In still other jurisdictions, social welfare agencies delay placing children with adoptive parents of the "wrong" race until efforts are undertaken to place the child with adoptive parents of the "right" race. Delay of any length is, of course, a cost in and of itself. While three months might seem like a negligible delay from the perspective of adults, such delays are lengthy indeed from the perspective of infants. Moreover, for many adults, children become less attractive as adoptees as they age. What seems at first like mere delay may obliterate the chance of some youngsters for adoption at all; prospective adoptive parents willing to adopt a child of six months may not be willing to adopt the same child at one year.

Furthermore, given that racial matching mirrors and reinforces the belief that same-race child placements are better and therefore preferable to transracial arrangements, some adults seeking to become foster or adoptive parents are likely to steer clear of transracial parenting. Some adults who would be willing to raise a child regardless of racial differences find themselves unwilling to do so in the face of social pressures that stigmatize transracial adoption as anything from second-best to cultural genocide. What this means in practice is that racial matching narrows the pool of prospective parents, which in turn either delays or prevents the transmission of children in need of parents to adults able and willing to serve as parents. How much misery this adds to our pained country is difficult to calibrate. That racial matching adds a substantial amount of misery, however, is inescapable.

The other level on which racial matching is disastrous has to do with its diffuse, long-term moral and political consequences. Racial matching reinforces racialism. It strengthens the baleful notion that race is destiny. It buttresses the notion that people of different racial backgrounds really are different in some moral, unbridgeable, permanent sense. It affirms the notion that race should be a cage to which people are assigned at birth and from which people should not be allowed to wander....

...

This does not mean that all racial criteria are illegitimate, only that all are presumptively illegitimate. Therefore, if racial criteria are to be used, the burden of persuasion rests on those in favor of using such criteria. Thus, in this context, the burden of persuasion rests not upon those who object to the use of racial criteria in making child placement decisions but rather upon those who wish to use such criteria. The burden of persuasion properly rests upon the proponents of racial matching, not those who contend, as I do, that race ought to play no part in child placement decisions.

There is no rationale sufficiently compelling to justify preferring same-race child placements over transracial placements. One asserted reason for favoring same-race placements (at least in terms of black children) is that African-American parents can, on average, better equip African-American children with what they will need to know in order to survive and prosper in a society that remains, in significant degree, a pigmentocracy. This rationale is doubly faulty.

First, it rests upon a racial generalization, a racial stereotype, regarding the relative abilities of white and black adults in terms of raising African-American children. Typically (and the exception does not apply here), our legal system rightly prohibits authorities from making decisions on the basis of racial generalizations, even if the generalizations are accurate. Our legal system demands that people be given individualized consideration to reflect and effectuate our desire to accord to each person respect as a unique and special individual. Thus, if an employer used whiteness as a criteria to prefer white candidates for a job on the grounds that, on average, white people have more access to education than black people, the employer would be in violation of an array of state and federal laws—even if the generalization used by the employer is accurate. We demand as a society a more exacting process, one more attentive to the surprising possibilities of individuals than the settled patterns of racial groups. Thus, even if one believes that, on average, black adults are better able than white adults to raise black children effectively, it would still be problematic to disadvantage white adults, on the basis of their race, in the selection process.

Second, there is no evidence that black foster or adoptive parents, on average, do better than white foster or adoptive parents in raising black children. The empirical basis for this claim is suspect; there are no serious, controlled, systematic studies that support it. Nor is this claim self-evidently persuasive. Those who confidently assert this claim rely on the hunch, accepted by many, that black adults, as victims of racial oppression, will generally know more than others about how best to instruct black youngsters on overcoming racial bias. A counter-hunch, however, with just as much plausibility, is that white adults, as insiders to the dominant racial group in America, will know more than racial minorities about the inner world of whites and how best to maneuver with and around them in order to advance one's interests in a white-dominated society.

To substantiate the claim that black adults will on average be better than white adults in terms of raising black children, one must stipulate a baseline conception of what constitutes correct parenting for a black child—otherwise, one will have no basis for judging who is doing better than whom.... There exists, however, no consensus on how best to raise a black child (or, for that matter, any other sort of child) or on what constitutes a proper sense of self worth or on what constitutes an appropriate racial identity or on how one would go about measuring any of these things. Is an appropriate sense of blackness evidenced by celebrating Kwanza, listening to rap, and seeking admission to Morehouse College? What about celebrating Christmas, listening to Mahalia Jackson, and seeking admission to Harvard? And what about believing in atheism, listening to Mozart, and seeking admission to Bard? Are any of these traits more or less appropriately black? And who should do the grading on what constitutes racial appropriateness? Louis Farrakhan? Jesse Jackson? Clarence Thomas?

Some moderate proponents of racial matching contend that, on average, white adults seeking foster or adoptive children will be less able than similarly situated black adults to tell these children how best to meet the racial impediments they will surely face. But what is the best advice to give? Blacks do not agree. Nor do whites. Again the key point is that there exists no consensus on how best to raise a black child or any other child.

In light of this lack of consensus, the tenuousness of our information regarding the relationship of racial status to social knowledge, the ever-growing complexity of our multicultural society, and our well-taken aversion to official racial distinctions in the absence of clear, strong justifications for them, our government should reject any scheme that engages expressly in racial steering on the basis of a hunch that certain people—because of their race, color, or national origin—will know better how to raise a child than other people of a different race, color, or national origin. If officials are satisfied that adults seeking foster or adoptive children are safe, sober folk, they should have to pass no racial screening. What parentless children need are not "white," "black," "yellow," "brown," or "red" parents but loving parents.

Yet another reason advanced in favor of moderate racial matching is that it may serve to save a child from placement in a transracial family setting in which the child will be made to feel uncomfortable by a disapproving surrounding community. It would be a regrettable concession, however, to allow bigotry to shape our law. One of the asserted justifications of segregation was that it protected blacks from the wrath of those whites who would strongly object to transracial public schooling and transracial accommodations in hotels and restaurants. When the New York Times editorializes today that "clearly, matching adoptive parents with children of the same race is a good idea," we should recall that not very long ago it was believed in some parts of this nation that "clearly" it was a good idea to match people of the same race in separate but equal parks, hospitals, prisons, cemeteries, telephone booths, train cars, and practically every other place one can imagine—all for the asserted purpose of accommodating the underlying racial sentiments of those who opposed "racial mixing."

...

This state of affairs is, quite simply, a political disaster—at least for integrationists like me who view the anti-racialist impulse of the civil rights movement circa 1963 as the great guiding sentiment around which struggles for racial justice should continue to cohere. Whether or not they recognize it, many liberals have abandoned their commitment to creating a society in which racial difference withers away into moral insignificance. Instead, often marching under the banner of "diversity," they have acquiesced to measures that are moving us toward a society in which one's racial background is deemed to have a definite, positive, moral meaning that the government officially recognizes, reinforces, and celebrates.

Many conservatives are also blameworthy. Some who merely tolerate the changes wrought by the civil rights revolution, because they can effectively do nothing about them, probably like the fact that racial matching is prevalent and may soon receive congressional approval; after all, racial matching validates to some degree the separatist intuitions that animated de jure segregation.

...

Unfortunately, one plausible explanation for this is that while they care intensely about the disadvantage imposed upon whites by preferential treatment in education and employment, they care little about the burdens imposed by racial matching, burdens that hurt everyone but that hurt racial minority children in particular.

... There is much to be done in order to create a more just, decent, and attractive society.

Key Websites

READERS' GUIDE TO ADOPTION-RELATED LITERATURE: TRANSRACIAL ADOPTION

This site provides a listing of nonfiction books about transracial adoption (which is here limited to the adoption of nonwhite children—i.e., black or Native American—by white adoptive parents). A related area is international adoption, which is included as a separate section.
http://members.aol.com/billgage/trnsracl.htm

MULTIETHNIC PLACEMENT ACT AND INTERETHNIC PLACEMENT PROVISIONS

The Multiethnic Placement Act (MEPA) and Interethnic Placement Provisions (IEP) were implemented in the spirit of removing barriers to permanency for the vast number of children in the child protective system, and to ensure that adoption and foster placements are not delayed or denied based on race, color, or national origin.
http://www.acf.dhhs.gov/programs/cb/special/mepaipp.htm

ADMINISTRATION FOR CHILDREN AND FAMILIES

The Administration for Children and Families (ACF), within the Department of Health and Human Services (HHS), is responsible for federal programs that promote the economic and social well-being of families, children, individuals, and communities. At this site, you can access ACF press releases and find additional information about Federal programs for children and their families.
http://www.acf.dhhs.gov/

ADOPTION AND THE AFRICAN-AMERICAN CHILD: A GUIDE FOR PARENTS

This website addresses the following issue areas: (1) Why is there a need for formal adoption of African-American children? (2) The 1960s and 1970s: A period of transition; (3) The 1980s and 1990s: Breaking the barriers; and (4) The African-American children who wait for adoption—what are the facts?
http://www.calib.com/naic/publications/aframpar.htm

BARRIERS TO SAME RACE PLACEMENT

Tom Gilles, M.A., and Joe Kroll, "Barriers to Same Race Placement," April 1991: The North American Council on Adoptable Children (NACAC) undertook this survey of 64 private and 23 public child placing agencies in 25 states during the fall of 1990 to add factual information to the debate. Answers to the survey's 42 questions shed light on placement practices and highlight policies and procedures most directly affecting minority adoption.
http://www.nysccc.org/T-Rarts/Barriers.html

SELECTED ARTICLES ON TRANSRACIAL/TRANSCULTURAL ADOPTION

This website provides a variety of articles, many from a first-person perspective.
http://www.nysccc.org/T-Rarts.html

AUDIO RECORDING OF TALK OF THE NATION PROGRAM
HEARD ON NATIONAL PUBLIC RADIO

The guests at this site examine why transracial adoption has ignited enormous controversy since the late 1960s and whether colorblind placement should be a priority or a last resort.
http://www.prognet.com/rafiles/npr/password/ne6d0501-3.ram

Does Racism Influence How the Death Penalty Is Applied?

A strong case can be made that racial minorities are being prosecuted under federal and state death penalty laws far beyond their proportion in the general population or the population of criminal offenders. Moreover, the number of prosecutions has been increasing over the past few years with no decline in the racial disparities. Many see this pattern of inequality as mounting evidence that race continues to play an unacceptable part in the application of capital punishment in America today. Others claim that this is too easy an interpretation of a complex issue.

Whether or not America's criminal justice system is biased against blacks today, it clearly was in the past. Between 1930 and 1964, for example, six southern jurisdictions—Louisiana, Mississippi, Oklahoma, Virginia, West Virginia, and the District of Columbia—put to death sixty-seven men for the crime of rape. Not one of the sixty-seven was white. All were black. Is it conceivable that not a single white man committed an equally serious rape in any of these places over a thirty-five-year period? Surely not.

Throughout American history, the death penalty has fallen disproportionately on racial minorities. For example, since 1930 nearly 90 percent of those executed for the crime of rape in this country were African Americans. Currently, about 50 percent of those on the nation's death rows are from minority populations representing 20 percent of the country's population.

In 1972, the U.S. Supreme Court overturned existing death penalty statutes in part because of the danger that those being selected to die were chosen out of racial prejudice. As the late Justice Douglas said in his concurrence overturning the death penalty:

> The discretion of judges and juries in imposing the death penalty enables the penalty to be selectively applied, feeding prejudices against the

accused if he is poor and despised, and lacking political clout, or if he is a member of a suspect and unpopular minority, and saving those who, by social position, may be in a more protected position.

The bulk of the evidence amassed since then on justice system bias is far less conclusive. Plenty of studies exist showing no bias in arrest, prosecution, adjudication, and sentencing. While plenty also exist that show possible evidence of bias, the general consensus among criminologists is that the evidence is not strong.

The Subcommittee on Civil and Constitutional Rights, in its report "Racial Disparities in Federal Death Penalty Prosecutions, 1988–1994," points out that race continues to plague the application of the death penalty in the United States. On the state level, racial disparities are most obvious in the predominant selection of cases involving white victims. On the federal level, cases selected have almost exclusively involved minority defendants.

The report notes that the federal government has long assumed the role of protecting against racially biased application of the law. But under the only active federal death penalty statute, the federal record of racial disparity has been even worse than that of the states.

Randall Kennedy, in "Race, Law, and Punishment," points out that those claiming that murderers of whites are punished more harshly than murderers of blacks use this information as a reason for abolishing the death penalty. He believes this does not make sense when most people favor capital punishment. Kennedy thinks the appropriate response should not be to abolish capital punishment, but to work to make sure more murderers of blacks are executed. Racial disparities in sentencing, he says, are being used as a smoke screen by those people who are against the death penalty.

Subcommittee on Civil and Constitutional Rights

Racial Disparities in Federal Death Penalty Prosecutions, 1988–1994

Twenty years have passed since this Court declared that the death penalty must be imposed fairly, and with reasonable consistency, or not at all, and, despite the effort of the states and courts to devise legal formulas and procedural rules to meet this daunting challenge, the death penalty remains fraught with arbitrariness, discrimination, caprice, and mistake.

—Justice Harry A. Blackmun, Feb. 22, 1994[1]

...

The Federal Death Penalty

Since the Supreme Court's 1972 decision in *Furman v. Georgia,*[3] the death penalty has been almost exclusively a state prerogative. Congress has so far not adopted the general sentencing procedures that would reinstate the federal death penalty. No federal executions have been carried out since 1963 and, until very recently, prosecutions under federal death penalty law were rare. But that began to change over the past few years, and can be expected to change dramatically if the House adopts pending legislation to restore generally—and expand—the federal death penalty.

In 1988, President Reagan signed the Anti-Drug Abuse Act. This legislation included a provision, sometimes referred to as the "drug kingpin" death penalty, which created an enforceable federal death penalty for murders committed by those involved in certain drug trafficking activities. The

From the U.S. Government Committee on the Judiciary, Staff Report by the Subcommittee on Civil and Constitutional Rights, March 1994. Case data provided by the Federal Death Penalty Resource Counsel Project, Columbia, SC.

death penalty provisions were added to the "continuing criminal enterprise" statute first enacted in 1984, 21 U.S.C. SS 848. The drug trafficking "enterprise" can consist of as few as five individuals, and even a low-ranking "foot soldier" in the organization can be charged with the death penalty if involved in a killing.

As the first enforceable federal death penalty adopted after *Furman*, SS 848 offers a forewarning as to how a general federal death penalty might be applied. This report, prepared with the assistance of the Death Penalty Information Center in Washington, D.C. and with case data from the Federal Death Penalty Resource Counsel Project, examines the application of SS 848.

Three-quarters of those convicted of participating in a drug enterprise under the general provisions of SS 848 have been white and only about 24 percent of the defendants have been black.[4] However, of those chosen for death penalty prosecutions under this section, just the opposite is true: 78 percent of the defendants have been black and only 11 percent of the defendants have been white. Although the number of homicide cases in the pool that the U.S. Attorneys are choosing from is not known (the Justice Department has not responded to Congressional inquiries for that data), the almost exclusive selection of minority defendants for the death penalty, and the sharp contrast between capital and non-capital prosecutions under SS 848, indicate a degree of racial bias in the imposition of the federal death penalty that exceeds even pre-*Furman* patterns.

Federal regulations require that local U.S. Attorneys obtain the personal written authorization of the Attorney General of the United States before proceeding with a capital prosecution. So far, former Attorneys General Thornburgh and Barr and present Attorney General Reno have approved capital prosecutions against a total of thirty-seven defendants under the 1988 "kingpin" law. Twenty-nine of the defendants have been black and four have been Hispanic. All ten of the defendants approved by Attorney General Reno for capital prosecution have been black. Judging by the death row populations of the states, no other jurisdiction comes close to this nearly 90 percent minority prosecution rate.[5]

Pace of Prosecutions Increasing

The pace of these prosecutions has been substantially increasing over the past two years. Although widely touted during the 1988 election year as a "tough" response to drug crime, there were only seven defendants prosecuted under this Act in the first three years after its passage and only one death sentence handed down. However, in 1992 alone, capital prosecutions against fourteen defendants were announced and another five death sentences resulted from these cases. Since January, 1993, sixteen more prosecutions have been announced.[6]

The underlying crimes for which these defendants are being prose-cuted are not excusable because the offenders are members of minorities. But the statistics raise the question of why these cases were chosen out of the large number of drug-related homicides over the past five years. By way of comparison, the proportion of African-Americans admitted to federal prison for all crimes has remained fairly constant between 21 percent and 27 percent during the 1980s, while whites accounted for approximately 75 percent of new federal prisoners.[7] Yet, when it comes to the federal death penalty, the scales dramatically tip the other way.

The federal government employed the death penalty for a variety of crimes prior to the 1972 *Furman* decision. But the racial breakdown was also just the opposite from current death penalty prosecutions. Between 1930 and 1972, 85 percent of those executed under federal law were white and 9 percent were black. The dramatic racial turnaround under the drug king-pin law clearly requires remedial action.

Although challenged at a Congressional hearing to provide an expla-nation for such racial disparities, and asked by the Chairman of this Subcommittee for data on potentially capital cases referred to Washington for approval by federal prosecutors, the Justice Department has offered no response.[8]

It is worth noting that some of the death penalty prosecutions under SS 848 have been against defendants who do not seem to fit the expected "drug kingpin" profile. In a number of cases, the U.S. Attorneys have sought the death penalty against young inner-city drug gang members and rela-tively small-time drug traffickers.[9] In other cases, the death penalty was returned against those directly involved in a murder, while the bosses who ordered the killings were given lesser sentences.[10]

Background on Race and the Death Penalty

Throughout American history, the death penalty has fallen disproportionate-ly on racial minorities. For example, since 1930 nearly 90 percent of those executed for the crime of rape in this country were African-Americans.[11] Currently, about 50 percent of those on the nation's death rows are from minority populations representing 20 percent of the country's population.

In 1972, the U.S. Supreme Court overturned existing death penalty statutes in part because of the danger that those being selected to die were chosen out of racial prejudice. As the late Justice Douglas said in his con-currence overturning the death penalty:

> [T]he discretion of judges and juries in imposing the death penalty enables the penalty to be selectively applied, feeding prejudices against the accused if he is poor and despised, and lacking political clout, or if he is a member of a suspect and unpopular minority, and saving those who, by social position, may be in a more protected position.[12]

Following the *Furman* decision, legislatures adopted death sentencing procedures that were supposed to eliminate the influence of race from the death sentencing process. However, evidence of racial discrimination in the application of capital punishment continues. Nearly 40 percent of those executed since 1976 have been black, even though blacks constitute only 12 percent of the population. And in almost every death penalty case, the race of the victim is white. Last year alone, 89 percent of the death sentences carried out involved white victims, even though 50 percent of the homicides in this country have black victims.[13] Of the 229 executions that have occurred since the death penalty was reinstated, only one has involved a white defendant for the murder of a black person.

Race of the victim discrimination was singled out by the U.S. General Accounting Office in its report "Death Penalty Sentencing" which concluded that studies showed:

> [The] race of the victim was found to influence the likelihood of being charged with capital murder or receiving the death penalty, i.e., those who murdered whites were found more likely to be sentenced to death than those who murdered blacks.[14]

This record of racial injustice played a significant part in Justice Harry Blackmun's recent decision to oppose the death penalty in every case. "Even under the most sophisticated death penalty statutes," said Blackmun, "race continues to play a major role in determining who shall live and who shall die."[15]

Conclusion

Race continues to plague the application of the death penalty in the United States. On the state level, racial disparities are most obvious in the predominant selection of cases involving white victims. On the federal level, cases selected have almost exclusively involved minority defendants.

Under our system, the federal government has long assumed the role of protecting against racially biased application of the law. But under the only active federal death penalty statute, the federal record of racial disparity has been even worse than that of the states. So far, the number of cases is relatively small compared to state capital prosecutions. However, the numbers are increasing, and under legislation currently being considered in Congress, the federal government would play a much wider role in death penalty prosecutions.

Notes

1. *Callins v. Collins*, No. 93-7054 (1994) (Blackmun, J., dissenting) (Supreme Court denial of review).

...

3. 408 U.S. 238 (1972).

4. U.S. Dept. of Justice, Bureau of Justice Statistics, *Special Report: Prosecuting Criminal Enterprises*, at 6, Table 10 (convictions 1987–90) (1993).

5. See NAACP Legal Defense Fund, Death Row, U.S.A., January 1994 (death rows by state with racial breakdowns).

6. Prosecutions against 10 defendants were approved by Attorney General Reno, including at least one in 1994. Prosecutions against 6 other defendants were approved in the previous Administration, but were not announced until June, 1993.

7. Bureau of Justice Statistics, *Sourcebook of Criminal Justice Statistics, 1991*, at table 6.78, p. 644 (1992).

8. On October 21, 1993, Rep. Melvin Watt (D-NC) asked then Deputy Attorney General Philip Heymann for an explanation of the racial disparities in capital prosecutions during the course of a House Judiciary Subcommittee hearing on the Administration's crime bill. Mr. Heymann promised a reply in two weeks. To date, Rep. Watt has received no response to his inquiry. Death Penalty Information Center phone conversation with Rep. Watt's office, Feb. 28, 1994. During the same hearing, Rep. Craig Washington (D-Tex.) remarked to Mr. Heymann that "if some redneck county in Texas had come up with figures like that, you'd been down there wanting to know why." See Federal Death Penalty Update, Newsletter of Federal Death Penalty Resource Counsel Project, January, 1994.

9. See, e.g., *United States v. Tipton et al.*, 3-92-CR68 (E.D. Va.) (prosecution of four young black inner-city gang members in Richmond, Va.); *United States v. Bilal Pretlow*, No. 90-CR-238 (D.N.J.) (a young black New Jersey gang member who committed suicide during his trial); *United States v. Chandler*, 996 F.2d 1073 (11th Cir. 1993) (prosecution of rural Alabama marijuana grower in murder-for-hire scheme).

10. See, e.g., *United States v. Hutching et al.*, No. CR-032-S (E.D. Okl.) (two "managers" of the drug enterprise received life sentences for murder while lower level defendant who was present at the murder was sentenced to death); *United States v. Michael Murray*, Cr. No. 1: CR-92-200 (M.D. Pa.) (Dept. of Justice reportedly declined to approve the U.S. Attorney's request to authorize the death penalty against the gang leader, Jonathan Bradley, whom the indictment alleges ordered the killing. A death sentence is being sought against Murray who was 19 years old at the time of the incident.). Information obtained from the Federal Death Penalty Resource Counsel Project report, Feb. 15, 1994.

11. U.S. Dept. of Justice, Bureau of Justice Statistics, Capital Punishment, 1981 (1982).

12. *Furman v. Georgia*, 92 S. Ct. 2726, 2735 (1972) (Douglas, J., concurring).

13. See, e.g., S. LaFraniere, FBI Finds Major Increase in Juvenile Violence in Past Decade, *Washington Post*, Aug. 30, 1992, at A13 (half of U.S. murder victims are black).

14. U.S. General Accounting Office, *Death Penalty Sentencing* 5 (Feb. 1990) (emphasis added).

15. *Callins v. Collins*, No. 93-7054 (1994) (Blackmun, J., dissenting).

No

Randall
Kennedy

Race, Law, and Punishment
The Death Penalty

···

If a jurisdiction tends to punish more harshly murderers of white than murderers of blacks, is the appropriate response to abolish capital punishment, to more narrowly limit the circumstances in which capital punishment is imposed, or to execute more people who murder blacks? Even if such a tendency exists, should it be the basis for granting relief to a convicted murderer who fails to show that racial discrimination affected the punishment meted out in his particular case? Is such a tendency a remediable wrong or, instead, an inevitable social trait whereby people unavoidably identify more with the victimization of "others"? If this tendency is a wrong, is remedying it within the capacity of courts or is remedying this wrong best left to the legislative and executive branches of government?

···

On May 13, 1978, Warren McCleskey, a black man, helped to rob the Dixie Furniture Store in Atlanta, Georgia. A white police officer, Frank Schlatt, attempted to foil the robbery but was killed by a shot to the head. Sometime later, McCleskey was arrested in connection with another armed robbery. Under questioning, he admitted to participating in the furniture store heist but denied shooting Officer Schlatt. After further investigation, it emerged that McCleskey had stolen a revolver capable of shooting the type of bullet that killed Officer Schlatt. McCleskey also reportedly admitted shooting Schlatt to both a codefendant and a neighboring inmate in jail, both of whom later testified against him.

A jury of eleven whites and one black sentenced McCluskey to life imprisonment for the robbery and death for the murder. His subsequent appeals followed the normal, dreary route of postconviction proceedings in capital cases. An aspect of his appeal, however, contained a challenge to the entire system of capital punishment in Georgia and beyond. Supported by the most comprehensive statistical analysis ever done on the racial demographics of sentencing in a single state, McCleskey's attorneys argued that their client's sentence should be invalidated because there was a constitutionally impermissible risk that both his race and that of his victim had played a significant role in the decision to sentence him to death.

McCleskey's claim was largely predicated on a study organized and overseen by David C. Baldus, an expert in the application of statistics to legal problems. The Baldus study was derived from records involving the disposition of more than two thousand murder cases between 1973 and 1979. The Georgia Department of Pardons and Paroles and other state agencies provided Baldus with police reports, parole board records, prison files, and other items that evidenced the process by which state authorities handled criminal homicides.

Three findings of the Baldus study are especially pertinent. First, viewing the evidence on a statewide basis, Baldus found "neither strong nor consistent" evidence of discrimination directed against black defendants because of their race. That did not prevent McCleskey's attorneys from asserting that "the race of the defendant—especially when the defendant is black and victim white—influences Georgia's capital sentencing process." In their argument to the Supreme Court, however, McCleskey's attorneys clearly subordinated the claim of race-of-the-defendant discrimination to the claim of race-of-the-victim discrimination.

Second, Baldus found that among the variables that might plausibly influence capital sentencing—age, level of education, criminal record, military record, method of killing, motive for killing, relationship of defendant to victim, strength of evidence, and so forth—the race of the victim emerged as the most consistent and powerful factor. Initially, simple correlations suggested the importance of this variable. Without attempting to control for the possible effects of competing variables, Baldus found that perpetrators in white-victim cases were eleven times more likely to be condemned to death than perpetrators in black-victim cases.

Professor Baldus and his associates subjected this striking correlation to extensive statistical analysis to test whether the seemingly racial nature of this disparity was explainable in terms of hidden factors confounded with race. He eventually took into account some 230 nonracial variables that might have influenced the pattern of sentencing. He concluded that even after accounting for every nonracial variable that might have mattered substantially, the race of the victim continued to have a statistically significant correlation with the imposition of capital sentences. Applying a statistical model that included the thirty-nine nonracial variables believed most likely to play a role in capital punishment in Georgia, the Baldus study concluded that the odds of being condemned to death were 4.3 times greater for defendants who killed whites than for defendants who killed blacks, a variable nearly as influential as a prior conviction for armed robbery, rape, or even murder.

Third, Baldus concluded that racial disparities in capital sentencing are most dramatic in that category containing neither the most aggravated nor the least aggravated homicides. Racial disparities are greatest, he argued, in the middle range of aggravated homicides. In the most aggravated cases, decisionmakers typically impose the death sentence regardless of racial variables, and in the least aggravated cases decisionmakers typically spare the defendant regardless of racial variables. In the middle range of aggravation, however, where a decision could go either way, the influence of racial variables emerges more powerfully. This hypothesis is particularly relevant to *McCleskey* because, in Baldus's view, McCleskey's crime was situated in the middle range of aggravated homicide.

After an evidentiary hearing, U.S. District Judge J. Owen Forrester rejected McCleskey's race discrimination claim primarily on the ground that the Baldus study did not represent "good statistical methodology." He objected to what he viewed as significant omissions, errors, and inconsistencies in Baldus's data base and inadequacies in the design of Baldus's statistical models. Judge Forrester's findings were subsequently eclipsed because the court of appeals and the Supreme Court resolved the case without reviewing them; the appellate courts assumed arguendo that the Baldus study was valid. Judge Forrester's findings, however, continue to be relevant insofar as much of the criticism of *McCleskey* and support for legislative responses to it is premised on a belief in the validity of the Baldus study.

Although a comprehensive examination of the Baldus study would itself require a volume, several considerations pertinent to making an independent evaluation should be mentioned. First, the Baldus study is a product of the death penalty abolitionist wing of the academic community. Although Professor Baldus maintains that he would have published the results of his study no matter what its conclusions, his study was partially financed by funds distributed by LDF—the employer of McCleskey's lawyers and an organization committed to erasing the death penalty. Baldus and his colleagues stated, moreover, that after a certain point, they began to conduct their research with litigation in mind. The Baldus study, in other words, is not the product of disinterested academic research subsequently used by a litigant's attorneys. Rather, the Baldus study is a species of sponsored research animated in part by sympathies with one side of a controversy. It should therefore be viewed with the skepticism that such research should always engender.

...

The factual core of the Baldus study withstands even a skeptical analysis, however. To some extent I am moved to this conclusion by the study's evident carefulness and its authors' insistence on making their data, premises, and calculations available and transparent to the public. I am also influenced by the sworn testimony of respected experts in Baldus's field, notwithstanding the risk of ideological taint identified above. The Baldus study, moreover, is consistent with findings published by a large body of prior research. Even commentators who generally deride allegations of racial discrimination in the administration of criminal law concede that in the context of capital punishment the race of the victim consistently influences sentencing decisions.

...

The Problem of Remedy

The central concern that dictated the Court's resolution of *McCleskey* was anxiety about what judges might have to face if it acknowledged that the influence of racial sentiment in sentencing represents a distortion and unfairness of constitutional dimension. Pretend for a moment, however, that the Supreme Court reversed the district court's rejection of the Baldus study and, based on the study's conclusions, declared a violation of the Equal Protection Clause. Assuming that the Court could have reached this point, what should it have done next?

One alternative would have been to abolish capital punishment entirely on the grounds that racial selectivity is an inextricable part of the administration of capital punishment in the United States and that it would be better to have no death penalty than one unavoidably influenced consistently by racial sentiment.

A more reserved variant would have involved vacating all death sentences in Georgia. Such a response would have fallen short of the ultimate aim of abolitionists since it would apply only to a single state. However, this response would surely have given a tremendous boost to the abolitionist movements by placing a large question mark over the legitimacy of any death penalty system generating unexplained racial disparities of the sort at issue in *McClesky*. Since studies suggest that *McClesky*-like statistics exist in several death penalty states, especially those with the largest death rows, the implementation of even a limited abolitionist remedy would have been significant indeed.

For those opposed to capital punishment anyway, abolishing it to vindicate the norms of equal protection is a costless enterprise. Abolition, however, is a costly prospect to the extent that one views the death penalty—as most Americans do—as a useful and highly valued public good. Polls indicate that, at least since the 1980s, upwards of 70 percent of Americans indicate that they favor capital punishment. Moreover, since 1988, the number of crimes punishable by death has increased dramatically, mainly as a result of federal legislation. From the perspective of a proponent of capital punishment, abolition as a remedy for race-of-the-victim discrimination is equivalent to reducing to darkness a town in which streetlights have been provided on a racially unequal basis. From this perspective, it would make more sense to remedy the inequality by installing lights in the parts of town which have been wrongly deprived of illumination. Carrying on the analogy, it would be better to remedy the problem outlined by the Baldus statistics by leveling up—increasing the number of people executed for murdering blacks—rather than leveling down—abolishing capital punishment altogether.

...

The Level-Up Solution to Racial Discrimination in Capital Sentencing

The level-up solution to the *McCleskey* problem would entail purposefully securing more death sentences against murderers of blacks. One way to pursue this aim would be to impose a choice upon jurisdictions with *McCleskey*-like sentencing patterns: Either respond as vigorously to the murders of blacks by condemning perpetrators of such crimes to death (as is done to murderers of whites), or relinquish the power to put anyone to death.

...

Another problem with the level-up alternative is that even those who favor, or at least tolerate, race-conscious remedies in some contexts reach a point where they find that such remedies are simply too severe to impose upon individuals who themselves played no direct part in inflicting the initial injury....

...

Race, Parochialism, and the Marketplace of Emotion

The statistics revealed by the Baldus study pose a difficult set of problems in part because Americans are deeply ambivalent about the social dynamics that give rise to these statistics. On the one hand, many subscribe to the idea that racial sentiments should play no role in social judgments. They say that they share the vision of a society in which people are judged solely on the quality of their character and not the color of their skin. On the other hand, many of these same people believe that it is proper for race to serve as a basis for pride, solidarity, loyalty, and affection. Every true man, Justice John Marshall Harlan declared, "has pride of race." That many people of all hues agree is illustrated by racially exclusive private clubs, racial selectivity in advertisements for companionship, demonstrations such as the Million Man March, and the entire gamut of cultural practices by which individuals, on a racial basis, prefer "their people" over others. It should come as no

surprise, then, that the enforcement of criminal law in jurisdictions dominated politically by whites would generate statistics suggesting that, in these
locales, officials respond more empathetically to white than black victims of
crime. That response is simply a reflection of a race-conscious society which
continually reproduces a racially stratified marketplace of emotion.

   This stratification stems from America's tragic history of race relations. It also stems, however, from a wider, perhaps even universal problem. Thousands of people die every day, yet most of us grieve only for those
few with whom we most identify: parents, children, siblings, spouses,
friends. In a sense, we all devalue the rest of the world in relation to our
own small circle of loved ones; hence Jean Jacques Rousseau's charge that
the preferences of friendship are "thefts" against humanity. Typically, when
we speak in sorrow about those killed in war, we refer to the casualties on
our side. When an airplane disaster occurs, local newspapers typically highlight only the lives of *local* victims. The *McCleskey* statistics, in other words,
do not represent something confined to race relations. Along many dimen-
sions, we all engage in differential valuations of human life according to
clannish criteria—family, locality, nationality. Recognizing the extent to
which the *McCleskey* problem is related to a universal dilemma in human
relations might help to facilitate a more candid discussion of this problem,
a discussion in which judges, legislators, and other influential policymakers might more easily acknowledge, reflect upon, and change the realities
of racial sentiment in American life.

Key Websites

THE DEATH PENALTY IN THE UNITED STATES

This site contains a brief history of the death penalty in the United States since 1930, when death penalty statistics began to be collected on a regular basis. This history emphasizes death penalty statistics and the constitutional history of the death penalty.

http://www.uaa.alaska.edu/just/death/history.html#unitedstates

SOURCES OF DEATH PENALTY STATISTICS

This site contains links to the most comprehensive sources of statistics on the death penalty in the United States.

http://www.uaa.alaska.edu/just/death/stats.html#sources

Executions by race of defendants executed:
http://www.essential.org/dpic/dpicrace.html

Race of death row inmates:
http://www.essential.org/dpic/dpicrace.html

THE DEBATE

This site provides a number of resources that present both sides of the death penalty debate in the United States. Views of law enforcement officers, as shown in a national poll of police executives and a resolution from a national police organization, are split on the death penalty. A selection of resources indicating positions on the death penalty from a religious perspective includes links to biblical citations and statements of officials, organizations, and individual adherents of different religious traditions, including Roman Catholicism, Protestantism, and Islam.

http://www.uaa.alaska.edu/just/death/debate.html#debate

ORGANIZATIONS AND SITES, PRO AND CON

This site gives links to organizations and web sites devoted to advocating either abolition or retention of the death penalty.

http://www.uaa.alaska.edu/just/death/procon.html#retention

RACIAL DISPARITIES IN FEDERAL DEATH PENALTY PROSECUTION, 1988–1994

Staff Report by the Subcommittee on Civil and Constitutional Rights, Committee on the Judiciary, One Hundred and Third Congress, Second Session, March 1994: This study analyzed the prosecutions under the federal

death penalty provisions of the Anti-Drug Abuse Act of 1988 and found that 89 percent of the defendants selected for capital prosecution were either African American or Mexican American.
http://www.essential.org/dpic/dpic.r05.html

THE DEATH PENALTY IN BLACK AND WHITE: WHO LIVES, WHO DIES, WHO DECIDES

Richard C. Dieter, Esq., "The Death Penalty in Black and White: Who Lives, Who Dies, Who Decides," June 1998: This report prepared by the executive director of an anti-death penalty group discusses two studies that claim to show that racism is present in the application of capital punishment.
http://www.essential.org/dpic/racerpt.html

Should the First Amendment Protect "Hate Speech" on College Campuses?

The United States grants more legal protection to freedom of speech than is even conceivable in most (and probably all) other democratic countries. Statements about public figures that other countries would think of as libelous are protected in the United States. The law provides for such broad protection of free speech because it is thought that only by protecting all forms of speech—whether a minority or majority position—will the public be assured of "uninhibited, robust, and wide-open debate." Protection is even applied to false statements about "private" people if those statements do not do any substantial harm. The U.S. Constitution even protects speech that other countries would restrict because it "could" threaten national security. In all these areas and more, U.S. law grants far greater protection to free expression than exists anywhere else in the world.

The area gets somewhat clouded when we consider hate speech. Even with the sense of uneasiness about hate speech that most people feel, such speech has received a significant amount of legal protection. People who favor tolerance of hate speech do not defend it because without it the public would sustain some grievous loss. On the contrary, hate speech is typically defended as the price society must pay in order to assure a system of free expression.

Between 1987 and 1992, hundreds of colleges and universities enacted codes of conduct that covered hate speech. An example of this is the code that the University of Pennsylvania passed in 1987 that forbade "any behavior, verbal or physical, that stigmatizes or victimizes individuals on the basis of race, ethnic or national origin ... and/or creates an intimidating or offensive academic, living, or work environment."

While some academic hate speech codes have been struck down by

Federal courts as patently illegal, or have been amended after coming under attack in the media or by students, many colleges and universities still have them.

The American Civil Liberties Union, in its briefing paper "Hate Speech on Campus," points out that the First Amendment to the U.S. Constitution protects speech no matter how offensive its content. Speech codes adopted by government-financed state colleges and universities amount to government censorship, in violation of the Constitution. And the ACLU believes that all campuses should adhere to First Amendment principles because academic freedom is a bedrock of education in a free society.

The briefing paper notes that "How much we value the right of free speech is put to its severest test when the speaker is someone we disagree with most. Speech that deeply offends our morality or is hostile to our way of life warrants the same constitutional protection as other speech because the right of free speech is indivisible: When one of us is denied this right, all of us are denied."

Charles R. Lawrence III disagrees, and, in his article "Is There Ever a Good Reason to Restrict Free Speech on a College Campus?—Yes," points out that we pay too little attention to the real victims of hate speech. He believes we have shown little understanding of their injury and that we have abandoned those whose race, gender, or sexual orientation continues to make them second-class citizens. He notes with sad irony that the first instinct of civil libertarians has been to challenge even the smallest, most narrowly framed efforts by universities to provide minority students with the protection they deserve.

American Civil
Liberties Union

Hate Speech on Campus

In recent years, a rise in verbal abuse and violence directed at people of color, lesbians and gay men, and other historically persecuted groups has plagued the United States. Among the settings of these expressions of intolerance are college and university campuses, where bias incidents have occurred sporadically since the mid-1980s. Outrage, indignation and demands for change have greeted such incidents—understandably, given the lack of racial and social diversity among students, faculty and administrators on most campuses.

Many universities, under pressure to respond to the concerns of those who are the objects of hate, have adopted codes or policies prohibiting speech that offends any group based on race, gender, ethnicity, religion or sexual orientation.

That's the wrong response, well-meaning or not. The First Amendment to the United States Constitution protects speech no matter how offensive its content. Speech codes adopted by government-financed state colleges and universities amount to government censorship, in violation of the Constitution. And the ACLU believes that all campuses should adhere to First Amendment principles because academic freedom is a bedrock of education in a free society.

How much we value the right of free speech is put to its severest test when the speaker is someone we disagree with most. Speech that deeply offends our morality or is hostile to our way of life warrants the same constitutional protection as other speech because the right of free speech is indivisible: When one of us is denied this right, all of us are denied. Since its founding in 1920, the ACLU has fought for the free expression of all ideas, popular or unpopular. That's the constitutional mandate.

From *Briefing Paper 16* (1996). Reprinted with the permission of the American Civil Liberties Union.

Where racist, sexist and homophobic speech is concerned, the ACLU believes that more speech—not less—is the best revenge. This is particularly true at universities, whose mission is to facilitate learning through open debate and study, and to enlighten. Speech codes are not the way to go on campuses, where all views are entitled to be heard, explored, supported or refuted. Besides, when hate is out in the open, people can see the problem. Then they can organize effectively to counter bad attitudes, possibly change them, and forge solidarity against the forces of intolerance.

College administrators may find speech codes attractive as a quick fix, but as one critic put it: "Verbal purity is not social change." Codes that punish bigoted speech treat only the symptom: The problem itself is bigotry. The ACLU believes that instead of opting for gestures that only appear to cure the disease, universities have to do the hard work of recruitment to increase faculty and student diversity; counseling to raise awareness about bigotry and its history, and changing curricula to institutionalize more inclusive approaches to all subject matter.

...

Q: Aren't some kinds of communication not protected under the First Amendment, like "fighting words?"

A: The U.S. Supreme Court did rule in 1942, in a case called *Chaplinsky v. New Hampshire*, that intimidating speech directed at a specific individual in a face-to-face confrontation amounts to "fighting words," and that the person engaging in such speech can be punished if "by their very utterance [the words] inflict injury or tend to incite an immediate breach of the peace." Say, a white student stops a black student on campus and utters a racial slur. In that one-on-one confrontation, which could easily come to blows, the offending student could be disciplined under the "fighting words" doctrine for racial harassment.

Over the past 50 years, however, the Court hasn't found the "fighting words" doctrine applicable in any of the hate speech cases that have come before it, since the incidents involved didn't meet the narrow criteria stated above. Ignoring that history, the folks who advocate campus speech codes try to stretch the doctrine's application to fit words or symbols that cause discomfort, offense or emotional pain.

Q: What about nonverbal symbols, like swastikas and burning crosses—are they constitutionally protected?

A: Symbols of hate are constitutionally protected if they're worn or displayed before a general audience in a public place—say, in a march or at a rally in a public park. But the First Amendment doesn't protect the use of nonverbal symbols to encroach upon, or desecrate, private property, such as burning a cross on someone's lawn or spray-painting a swastika on the wall of a synagogue or dorm.

In its 1992 decision in *R.A.V. v. St. Paul,* the Supreme Court struck down as unconstitutional a city ordinance that prohibited cross-burnings based on their symbolism, which the ordinance said makes many people feel "anger, alarm or resentment." Instead of prosecuting the cross-burner for the content of his act, the city government could have rightfully tried him under criminal trespass and/or harassment laws.

The Supreme Court has ruled that symbolic expression, whether swastikas, burning crosses or, for that matter, peace signs, is protected by the First Amendment because it's "closely akin to 'pure speech.'" That phrase comes from a landmark 1969 decision in which the Court held that public school students could wear black armbands in school to protest the Vietnam War. And in another landmark ruling, in 1989, the Court upheld the right of an individual to burn the American flag in public as a symbolic expression of disagreement with government policies.

Q: Aren't speech codes on college campuses an effective way to combat bias against people of color, women and gays?

A: Historically, defamation laws or codes have proven ineffective at best and counter-productive at worst. For one thing, depending on how they're interpreted and enforced, they can actually work against the interests of the people they were ostensibly created to protect. Why? Because the ultimate power to decide what speech is offensive and to whom rests with the authorities—the government or a college administration—not with those who are the alleged victims of hate speech.

In Great Britain, for example, a Racial Relations Act was adopted in 1965 to outlaw racist defamation. But throughout its existence, the Act has largely been used to persecute activists of color, trade unionists and anti-nuclear protesters, while the racists—often white members of Parliament—have gone unpunished.

Similarly, under a speech code in effect at the University of Michigan for 18 months, white students in 20 cases charged black students with offensive speech. One of the cases resulted in the punishment of a black student for using the term "white trash" in conversation with a white student. The code was struck down as unconstitutional in 1989 and, to date, the ACLU has brought successful legal challenges against speech codes at the Universities of Connecticut, Michigan and Wisconsin.

These examples demonstrate that speech codes don't really serve the interests of persecuted groups. The First Amendment does. As one African American educator observed: "I have always felt as a minority person that we have to protect the rights of all because if we infringe on the rights of any persons, we'll be next."

Q: But don't speech codes send a strong message to campus bigots, telling them their views are unacceptable?

A: Bigoted speech is symptomatic of a huge problem in our country; it is not the problem itself. Everybody, when they come to college, brings with them the values, biases and assumptions they learned while growing up in society, so it's unrealistic to think that punishing speech is going to rid campuses of the attitudes that gave rise to the speech in the first place. Banning bigoted speech won't end bigotry, even if it might chill some of the crudest expressions. The mindset that produced the speech lives on and may even reassert itself in more virulent forms.

Speech codes, by simply deterring students from saying out loud what they will continue to think in private, merely drive biases underground where they can't be addressed. In 1990, when Brown University expelled a student for shouting racist epithets one night on the campus, the institution accomplished nothing in the way of exposing the bankruptcy of racist ideas.

Q: Does the ACLU make a distinction between speech and conduct?

A: Yes. The ACLU believes that hate speech stops being just speech and becomes conduct when it targets a particular individual, and when it forms a pattern of behavior that interferes with a student's ability to exercise his or her right to participate fully in the life of the university.

The ACLU isn't opposed to regulations that penalize acts of violence, harassment or intimidation, and invasions of privacy. On the contrary, we believe that kind of conduct should be punished. Furthermore, the ACLU recognizes that the mere presence of speech as one element in an act of violence, harassment, intimidation or privacy invasion doesn't immunize that act from punishment. For example, threatening, bias-inspired phone calls to a student's dorm room, or white students shouting racist epithets at a woman of color as they follow her across campus—these are clearly punishable acts.

Several universities have initiated policies that both support free speech and counter discriminatory conduct. Arizona State, for example, formed a "Campus Environment Team" that acts as an education, information and referral service. The team of specially trained faculty, students and administrators works to foster an environment in which discriminatory harassment is less likely to occur, while also safeguarding academic freedom and freedom of speech.

Q: Well, given that speech codes are a threat to the First Amendment, and given the importance of equal opportunity in education, what type of campus policy on hate speech would the ACLU support?

A: The ACLU believes that the best way to combat hate speech on campus is through an educational approach that includes counter-speech, workshops on bigotry and its role in American and world history, and real—not superficial—institutional change.

Universities are obligated to create an environment that fosters tolerance and mutual respect among members of the campus community, an environment in which all students can exercise their right to participate fully in campus life without being discriminated against. Campus administrators on the highest level should, therefore,

■ speak out loudly and clearly against expressions of racist, sexist, homophobic and other bias, and react promptly and firmly to acts of discriminatory harassment;

- create forums and workshops to raise awareness and promote dialogue on issues of race, sex and sexual orientation;
- intensify their efforts to recruit members of racial minorities on student, faculty and administrative levels;
- and reform their institutions' curricula to reflect the diversity of peoples and cultures that have contributed to human knowledge and society, in the United States and throughout the world.

ACLU Executive Director Ira Glasser stated, in a speech at the City College of New York: "There is no clash between the constitutional right of free speech and equality. Both are crucial to society. Universities ought to stop restricting speech and start teaching."

Is There Ever a Good Reason to Restrict Free Speech on a College Campus?—Yes

Charles R. Lawrence III

I have spent the better part of my life as a dissenter. As a high school student, I was threatened with suspension for refusing to participate in a civil defense drill, and I have been a conspicuous consumer of my First Amendment liberties ever since. There are very strong reasons for protecting even speech that is racist. Perhaps the most important is that such protection reinforces our society's commitment to tolerance as a value. By protecting bad speech from government regulation, we are forced to combat it as a community.

I am, however, deeply apprehensive about the resurgence of racial violence and the corresponding increase in the incidence of verbal and symbolic assault and harassment to which blacks and other traditionally excluded groups are subjected. I am troubled by the way the debate has been framed in response to the recent surge of racist incidents on college and university campuses and in response to some universities' attempts to regulate harassing speech. The problem has been framed as one in which the liberty of free speech is in conflict with the elimination of racism. I believe this has placed the bigot on the moral high ground and fanned the rising flames of racism.

Above all, I am troubled that we have not listened to the real victims—that we have shown so little understanding of their injury, and that we have abandoned those whose race, gender or sexual orientation continues to make them second-class citizens. It seems to me a very sad irony that the first instinct of civil libertarians has been to challenge even the smallest, most narrowly framed efforts by universities to provide minority students with the protection that the Constitution, in my opinion, guarantees them.

The landmark 1954 case of *Brown vs. Board of Education* is not about speech. But *Brown* can be broadly read as articulating the principle of equal citizenship. *Brown* held that segregated schools were inherently unequal because of the message that segregation conveyed: that black children were an untouchable caste, unfit to go to school with white children. If we understand the necessity of eliminating the system of signs and symbols that signal the inferiority of blacks, then we should hesitate before proclaiming that all racist speech that stops short of physical violence must be defended.

University officials who have formulated policies to respond to incidents of racial harassment have been characterized in the press as "thought police," even though such policies generally do nothing more than impose sanctions against intentional face-to-face insults. Racist speech that takes the form of such insults, catcalls or other assaultive speech aimed at an individual or small group of persons falls directly within the "fighting words" exception to First Amendment protection. The Supreme Court has held in *Chaplinsky vs. New Hampshire* that words which "by their very utterance inflict injury or tend to incite an immediate breach of the peace" are not protected by the First Amendment.

If the purpose of the First Amendment is to foster the greatest amount of speech, racial insults disserve that purpose. Assaultive racist speech functions as a pre-emptive strike. The invective is experienced as a blow, not as a proffered idea. And once the blow is struck, a dialogue is unlikely to follow. Racial insults are particularly undeserving of First Amendment protection, because the perpetrator's intention is not to discover truth or initiate dialogue but to injure the victim. In most situations, members of minority groups realize that they are likely to lose if they fight back, and are forced to remain silent and submissive.

Courts have held that offensive speech may not be regulated in public forums (such as streets, where the listener may avoid the speech by moving on). But the regulation of otherwise protected speech has been permitted when the speech invades the privacy of the unwilling listener's home, or when the unwilling listener cannot avoid the speech. Racist posters, flyers and graffiti in dormitories, bathrooms and other common living spaces would seem to fall within the reasoning of these cases. Minority students should not be required to remain in their rooms in order to avoid racial insult. Minimally, they should find a safe haven in their dorms and in all other common rooms that are a part of their daily routine.

I would also argue that the university's responsibility to give these students an equal educational opportunity provides a compelling justification for regulations that ensure them safe passage in all common areas. A minority student should not have to risk becoming the target of racially assaulting speech every time he or she chooses to walk across campus. Regulating vilifying speech that cannot be anticipated or avoided need not preclude announced speeches and rallies—situations that would give minority group members and their allies the opportunity to organize counterdemonstrations or avoid the speech altogether.

The most commonly advanced argument against the regulation of racist speech proceeds something like this: We recognize that minority groups suffer pain and injury as the result of racist speech, but we must allow this hate-mongering for the benefit of society as a whole. Freedom of speech is the life blood of our democratic system. It is especially important for minorities, because often it is their only vehicle for rallying support for the redress of their grievances. It will be impossible to formulate a prohibition so precise that it will prevent the racist speech you want to suppress, without catching in the same net all kinds of speech that it would be unconscionable for a democratic society to suppress.

Such arguments seek to strike a balance between our concern, on the one hand, for the continued free flow of ideas and the democratic process dependent on that flow, and, on the other, our desire to further the cause of equality. There can, however, be no meaningful discussion of reconciling these two values until it is acknowledged that racist speech inflicts real harm, and that this harm is far from trivial.

To engage in a debate about the First Amendment and racist speech without a full understanding of the nature and extent of that harm is to risk making the First Amendment an instrument of domination rather than a vehicle of liberation. We have not all known the experience of victimization by racist, misogynist and homophobic speech, nor do we equally share the burden of the harm it inflicts. We are often quick to say that we have heard the cry of the victims when we have not.

The *Brown* case is again instructive, because it speaks directly to the psychic injury inflicted by racist speech by noting that the symbolic message of segregation affected "the hearts and minds" of Negro children "in a way unlikely ever to be undone." Racial epithets and harassment often cause deep emotional scarring and feelings of anxiety and fear that pervade every aspect of a victim's life.

Brown also recognized that black children did not have an equal opportunity to learn and participate in the school community when they were subjected to the humiliation and psychic assault contained in the message of segregation. University students bear an analogous burden when they are forced to live and work in an environment where at any moment they may be subjected to denigrating verbal harassment and assault. The same injury was addressed by the Supreme Court when it held that, under Title VII of the Civil Rights Act of 1964, sexual harassment that creates a hostile or abusive work environment violates the ban on sex discrimination in employment.

Carefully drafted university regulations could bar the use of words as assault weapons while leaving unregulated even the most heinous of ideas, provided those ideas are presented at times and places and in manners that leave an opportunity for reasoned rebuttal or escape from immediate insult.

The history of the development of the right to free speech has been one of carefully evaluating the importance of free expression and its effects on other important societal interests. We have drawn the line between protected and unprotected speech before without dire results. (Courts have, for example, exempted from the protection of the First Amendment obscene speech and speech that disseminates official secrets, defames or libels another person, or is used to form a conspiracy or monopoly.

Blacks and other people of color are skeptical about the argument that even the most injurious speech must remain unregulated because, in an unregulated marketplace of ideas, the best ideas will rise to the top and gain acceptance. Experience tells quite the opposite. People of color have seen too many demagogues elected by appealing to America's racism, and too many sympathetic politicians shy away from issues that might brand them as too closely allied with disparaged groups.

Whenever we decide that the racist speech must be tolerated because of the importance of maintaining societal tolerance for all unpopular speech, we are asking blacks and other subordinated groups to bear the burden for the good of all. We must be careful that the ease with which we strike the balance against the regulation of racist speech is in no way influenced by the fact that the cost will be borne by others. We must be certain that those who will pay that price are fairly represented in our deliberations and that they are heard.

At the core of the argument that we should resist all government regulation of speech is the ideal that the best cure for bad speech is good—that ideas that affirm equality and the worth of all individuals will ultimately prevail. This is an empty ideal unless those of us who would fight racism are vigilant and unequivocal in that fight. We must look for ways to assist students whose speech and political participation are chilled in a climate of racial harassment.

Civil rights lawyers might consider suing on behalf of blacks whose right to an equal education is denied by a university's failure to ensure a nondiscriminatory educational climate or conditions of employment. We must develop a First Amendment jurisprudence grounded in the reality of our history and our contemporary experience. We must think hard about how best to launch legal attacks against the most indefensible forms of hate speech. Good lawyers can create exceptions and narrow interpretations that limit the harm of hate speech without opening the floodgates of censorship.

Everyone concerned with these issues must find ways to engage actively in actions that resist and counter the racist ideas that we would have the First Amendment protect. If we fail in this, the victims of hate speech must rightly assume that we are on the bigots' side.

KEY WEBSITES

FACULTY ATTITUDES TOWARD REGULATING SPEECH ON COLLEGE CAMPUSES

Eric L. Dey and Sylvia Hurtado, "Faculty Attitudes toward Regulating Speech on College Campuses": In this study the authors examine faculty support for different policies designed to regulate certain aspects of speech on campus. Their goal is to highlight the underlying contradictions and complexities associated with faculty attitudes toward campus speech policies.
http://muse.jhu.edu/demo/rhe/20.1dey.html

ACADEMIC FREEDOM VS. CIVIL RIGHTS

Craig R. Smith and Peirce R. Moser, "Academic Freedom vs. Civil Rights," Center for First Amendment Studies, California State University, Long Beach: This study examines the tension between academic freedom and civil rights with an eye to sorting out the proper uses of the First Amendment on campuses versus the misuse of this sacred right. It looks at academic freedom from several perspectives: first, a historical review of court decisions shaping the current doctrine of academic freedom; second, an examination of the reigning case law concerning both individuals and institutions; and third, a look at the shifting burdens of proof that have created confusion in recent cases involving academic freedom.
http://www.csulb.edu/~research/Cent/Amend/acadfree.html

WAR OF WORDS: SPEECH CODES AT COLLEGES
AND UNIVERSITIES IN THE UNITED STATES

Arati Korwar, "War of Words: Speech Codes at Colleges and Universities in the United States," Freedom Forum First Amendment Center, Nashville, Tennessee: This report examines speech codes at both public and private universities and colleges throughout the United States today. It looks not only at the codes that specifically prohibit expression aimed at members of minority groups and women, but also at a whole array of regulations affecting campus expression. The study examines the two sides of the issue and summarizes the relevant case law affecting campus speech codes.
http://www.fac.org/publicat/warwords/warofwrd.htm

HATE CRIMES, 1995

U.S. Department of Justice, Federal Bureau of Investigation, Criminal Justice Information Services (CJIS) Division, Uniform Crime Reports, Hate Crimes, 1995: Preliminary figures show 7,947 hate crime incidents were reported to the FBI during 1995. The incidents were reported by more than 9,500 law enforcement agencies in 45 states and the District of Columbia, covering 75 percent of the U.S. population. This site will lead you to data from later years as they become available.
http://www.fbi.gov/ucr/hatecm.htm

Has Racism Become a Thing of the Past?

In 1940, black sociologist W. E. B. Du Bois wrote his autobiography, in which he looked back on a half-century of civil rights activity. He was far from optimistic about the future of race relations. He felt that all the major strategies for black advancement had failed miserably. He thought Booker T. Washington's message to black leaders that they should concentrate more on education and less on civil rights had also failed. In addition, the NAACP's fight for equal rights and an end to segregation, in which Du Bois himself had played a leading role, had produced few results. Du Bois reluctantly concluded that for many years or even generations into the future the racial scene would not improve.

Despite Du Bois's dismal predictions, the 1940s and 1950s saw blacks engaging in a major population shift. Millions left the South for the freer environment provided by the North. At the same time, millions more moved from the southern countryside to southern cities, where opportunities for organization and action were much greater. This migration provided the groundwork for the civil rights movement and the resulting changes in race relations.

The economic gap between whites and blacks also narrowed during this period. In 1940, 43 percent of all black men worked in agriculture as farm laborers or sharecroppers at terribly low salaries. Sixty percent of black women worked as domestic servants. The migration produced an improvement in the kinds of jobs African Americans could find and the level of pay they could receive.

Sociologist Orlando Patterson, in "Progress and Resentment in America's 'Racial' Crisis," argues that racism has declined enough that African Americans are now very much a part of the nation's political, economic, and cultural life. They have served as governors, senators, and powerful congressman. He believes being black is no longer a significant obstacle to participation in the public life of the United States.

Law professors Charles R. Lawrence III and Mari J. Matsuda disagree. In "We Won't Go Back," they note that racism is alive and well in America. They point to a variety of survey findings that a significant number of whites believe that blacks are more prone to violence than other racial groups, prefer welfare over work, are less ambitious, and are not as hardworking as other groups. Whites also believe that blacks do not take care of their children as well as other races and are less intelligent. They point out that as long as these views are still prevalent we are a long way off from declaring racism a thing of the past.

Progress and Resentment
in America's "Racial" Crisis

Orlando
Patterson

...

... There is no denying the fact that, in absolute terms, Afro-Americans, on average, are better off now than at any other time in their history. The civil rights movement effectively abolished the culture of postjuridical slavery, which, reinforced by racism and legalized segregation, had denied Afro-American people the basic rights of citizenship in the land of their birth.

Afro-Americans are now very much a part of the nation's political life, occupying positions in numbers and importance that go well beyond mere ethnic representation or tokenism. Quite apart from the thousands of local and appointed officials around the country—several having served as mayors of the nation's largest cities—Afro-Americans have held positions of major national importance in what is now the dominant power in the world. They have served as governors, senators, and powerful congressmembers chairing major House committees, and as appointed officials filling some of the most important offices in the nation, including that of the head of the most powerful military machine on earth. In 1995 the Colin Powell phenomenon bedazzled the nation, and with his high-profile appointment as chairman of the national campaign to encourage volunteers to help children there is renewed speculation about his candidacy in 2000. For the first time in American political history, an Afro-American is seriously under consideration for the nation's highest office, with his strongest support coming from quarters often considered conservative on ethnicity.

It would be ridiculous to dismiss these developments as aberrations. What they demonstrate, beyond a doubt, is that being Afro-American is no longer a significant obstacle to participation in the public life of the nation.

What is more, Afro-Americans have also become full members of what may be called the nation's moral community and cultural life. They are no longer in the basement of moral discourse in American life, as was the case up to about forty years ago. Until then Afro-Americans were socially "invisible men" in the nation's consciousness, a truly debased ex-slave people. America was assumed to be a Euro-American country. The mainstream media, the literary and artistic communities, the great national debates about major issues, even those concerning poverty, simply excluded Afro-Americans from consideration in spite of the contributions they had made to the nation's cultural life.

No longer. The enormity of the achievement of the last forty years in American ethnic relations cannot be overstated. For better or worse, the Afro-American presence in American life and thought is today pervasive. A mere 13 percent of the population, Afro-Americans dominate the nation's popular culture: its music, its dance, its talk, its sports, its youth fashion; and they are a powerful force in its popular and elite literatures. "American culture," as Albert Murray insisted a quarter of a century ago, "even in its most rigidly segregated precincts, is patently and irrevocably composite ... incontestably mulatto." An Afro-American music, jazz, is the nation's classical voice, defining, audibly, its entire civilizational style. So powerful and unavoidable is the Afro-American popular influence that it is now common to find people who, while remaining racists in personal relations and attitudes, nonetheless have surrendered their tastes, and much of their viewing and listening time, to Afro-American entertainers, talk-show hosts, and sit-com stars. The typical Oprah Winfrey viewer is a conservative Euro-American, lower-middle-class housewife, and 66 percent of all Americans are of the belief that she is either "somewhat likely" or "very likely" to go to heaven, a state of cherishment exceeded only by Mother Teresa in the hearts of her fellow Americans. Among the young, the typical rap fan is an upper-middle-class, Euro-American suburban youth and Michael Jordan the ultimate hero.

...

Most of these developments were facilitated by another revolution in Afro-American life: the rapid growth in school enrollment and educational achievement at all levels. In 1940 there was a four-year gap in median years of schooling between Euro-Americans and Afro-Americans; by 1995 this gap had been reduced to a few months. During the same period ... Afro-Americans in the ages 25 to 29 years almost eliminated the gap with Euro-Americans in the proportion completing high school, up from 12.3 percent to 86.5 percent, compared to the Euro-American improvement from 41.2

percent up to 87.4 percent. These dramatic improvements are not restricted to the youngest cohorts. Nearly three-quarters of all Afro-Americans over age 25 have had at least a high school education.

...

Of greater immediate concern are developments in higher education. After rapid increases during the 1970s in college completion among Afro-Americans, the numbers fell off during the eighties, especially among men. Afro-American women are now graduating from college at twice the rate of Afro-American men, and the gender differences in graduation rates are even greater for graduate and professional schools. The long-term effect has been that while the proportion of Afro-Americans over 25 years of age completing college has grown from under 1.5 percent in 1940 to almost 13 percent in 1995, this is still barely over half of the Euro-American rate of 24 percent.

Even so, a tenfold increase in college completion is nothing to be sniffed at. Such great absolute progress constitutes a significant narrowing of the gap between the two groups, the Euro-American college completion rate having grown less than fivefold since the forties. Afro-Americans, from a condition of mass illiteracy fifty years ago, are now among the most educated groups of people in the world, with median years of schooling and college completion rates higher than those of most European nations. Although some readers may think this observation is a shocking observation, it is not. It is a fact. It only sounds like an overstatement when heard against the din of the liberal advocacy community's insistence that the miseducation of Afro-Americans is the major source of their present dilemmas.

This extraordinary growth in educational attainment largely accounts for another great change in the condition of Afro-Americans. The rise of a genuine Afro-American middle class in recent decades is cause for celebration, although no one is more inclined to belittle the fact than members of the Afro-American establishment itself. What used to be called dismissively "the *Afro-American* middle class" meant those Afro-American persons who happened to be at the top of the bottom rung: Pullman porters, headwaiters, successful barbers and streetfront preachers, small-time funeral parlor owners and the like. Today the term *Afro-American middle class* means that segment of the *nation's* middle class that happens to be Afro-American, and it is no longer dependent on a segregated economy. What the economists James P. Smith and Finis R. Welch wrote in 1986 remains true today: "The real story of the last forty years has been the emergence of the black middle class, whose income gains have been real and substantial. The growth in the size of the black middle class was so spectacular that as a group it outnumbers the black poor. Finally, for the first time in American history, a sizable number of black men are economically better off than white middle-class America. During the last twenty years alone, the odds of a black man penetrating the ranks of the economic elite increased tenfold."

···

Nearly all sociologists take into account educational and occupational factors when arriving at an estimate of the size of the middle class. My own calculations, using this approach, show that at least 35 percent of Afro-American adult, male workers are solidly middle class. The percentage is roughly the same for adult female workers who, while they earn less than their male counterparts, are in white-collar occupations to a much greater extent.

Liberal critics of this generally positive interpretation of middle-class developments like to bemoan what they consider the fragile economic base of newly arrived Afro-Americans. Sharon M. Collins, in an informative study of Afro-American corporate executives, emphasizes "the dependency and the fragility" of this elite group of Afro-Americans, which she attributes to their "politically mediated opportunity structure." She warns that the size of the group faces erosion in the absence of a sympathetic political environment. Apart from the fact that this is hardly a flattering view of the abilities of Afro-American executives, it flies in the face of clear evidence that their fortunes have not declined during periods of conservative Republican ascendancy.

···

While these ethnic comparisons are important, we should be careful not to exaggerate them by concentrating too heavily on aggregate measurements. In America, and throughout the world, being middle class means having stable familial arrangements, whether they be East Indian extended families initiated by arranged marriages, Chinese clans, patriarchal Middle Eastern polygamous households, Icelandic common-law unions, California gay companionships, or standard married couple families. The important common feature is that they are usually enduring social units based on moderately stable unions in which at least two adults pool resources and skills to sustain a mutually desired lifestyle and to provide a structured, enriching environment for the reproduction and socialization of children who will become competent, middle-class adults. If we are to compare meaningfully the progress made by Afro-Americans in closing the gap with Euro-Americans, we should take into account this fundamental feature of middle-class life—otherwise, we are comparing sociological apples with pineapples.

What do we find when such meaningful comparisons are made? The results are striking.... [I]n sharp contrast to the failure to close the ethnic family income gap when all families are indiscriminately compared, we find that the median income of Afro-American families headed by a married couple was $41,307 in 1995, which was 87 percent of that earned by similar Euro-American families. This marked a stunning improvement in both absolute and relative terms for such Afro-American families that, in 1967, earned only 68 percent of their Euro-American counterparts. We find the same impressive relative and absolute improvements when we compare individuals working full-time. The median earnings of Afro-American men working year-round and full-time went up from $20,056 in 1967 to $24,428 in constant (1995) dollars, jumping from 64 percent to 75 percent of Euro-American earnings. And, in the most dramatic improvement of all, the year-round full-time earnings of Afro-American women increased from $13,410 in 1967 to $20,665 in 1995—from 74.6 percent to 90 percent of Euro-American women's earnings. Indeed, the most recent data bring even more extraordinary news about the progress of Afro-American women. For the first time in American history, a significant category of Afro-American workers now earns more than their Euro-American counterparts: As of March 1993, the nation's 1,025,000 Afro-American women who held a bachelor's degree or higher reported median annual earnings of $27,745, compared with earnings of $26,356 by Euro-American women with the same educational attainment.

...

We Won't Go Back

Charles R.
Lawrence III
and Mari J.
Matsuda

...

The assumption that Americans are no longer racist is central to the argument against race-based affirmative action. Opponents of affirmative action proclaim that we have won the war against bigotry and achieved a society that is essentially free of racial prejudice. Slavery, the genocide of native populations, segregation, the wartime incarceration of Japanese American citizens, are all distant memories, unfortunate blemishes on an otherwise glorious history. If there was a time when some significant number of us were bigots, the argument goes, that time is long past, and none of us is responsible for crimes committed before we were born. Certainly, critics concede, a small number of practicing racists remain, but they are social outlaws in a society committed to racial equality, outlaws subject to strong antidiscrimination laws as well as social sanction. In this book, we call this argument the Big Lie.

Some of our most influential political voices have eagerly promoted such notions. Robert Dole attacks affirmative action on the ground that slavery occurred "before we were born," and future generations ought not to have to continue "paying a price" for ancient wrongs. Newt Gingrich dismisses affirmative action by asserting that the long history of discrimination against African Americans is no different from that faced by white ethnic groups. "Virtually every American" has been subjected to discrimination, he argues.

The Big Lie is indispensable to the argument against affirmative action. If we believe that we have eradicated most of America's racism, there is no

111

need for a remedy that takes racism into account. If there are no racist employers, then there is no need for government-mandated set-asides to ensure that those employers hire minorities. If the differences between whites and blacks in educational achievement and test scores are not reflective of continuing racial barriers to educational opportunity, then there is no need for minority admissions programs. If the playing field is already level, then affirmative action is no longer a remedy required by morality and justice. It becomes "reverse discrimination," "preferential treatment," and "racial entitlement." Only when such deceits are believed can affirmative action be turned on its head to become racism itself.

...

Racism is alive and well in America, shaping our suburban geography and weaving through our private conversations. Recent polls confirm what we know from experience: Racist attitudes persist in the 1990s. In a National Research Center survey conducted between February and April 1990, a majority of whites questioned said they believe Blacks and Hispanics are likely to prefer welfare to hard work and tend to be lazier than whites, more prone to violence, less intelligent, and less patriotic.

A June 1993 Anti-Defamation League survey found similar disenchanting results. A significant number of whites reported their belief that Blacks are more prone to violence than other racial groups, prefer welfare over work, are less ambitious, are loud and pushy, and are not as hardworking as other groups. Somewhat smaller numbers of respondents said that Blacks do not take care of their children as well as people of other races, and have too much power in the United States. An especially disturbing revelation in this study was the finding that young people under thirty were more apt to hold racist attitudes than people between thirty and fifty.

The sentiments reflected in these surveys were echoed by whites who participated in two focus groups sponsored by People for the American Way in December of 1991. The members of the groups were randomly selected young people between eighteen and twenty-four years old. They responded to questions and engaged one another in discussion while a professional pollster observed them through a one-way mirror. Promised anonymity, they criticized and ridiculed Blacks and frankly discussed feelings of revulsion toward them. While a few participants challenged the racial stereotypes offered by others, most went along with the group consensus. They believed Blacks do not have a work ethic, have too many children, and work less hard than whites. One man said that "blacks are fundamentally different" and he "does not like to associate with them." Another said, "They're just different. It's kind of bad to say, but I mean they do have an odor that's different from white people unless they cover it up with a deodorant or cologne or something of that nature. You know, their hair is different.... It's just that I don't seek interest in these people and don't think I'm prejudiced because of that."

...

The most recent decade has also seen a significant rise in the number of hate crimes motivated by racial bias. In 1994 there were 1,637 Black victims of hate violence and 274 racially motivated offenses against Asian Americans. Racist hate groups such as the Ku Klux Klan have witnessed an alarming increase in membership; the KKK alone grew from 11,000 in 1981 to 22,000 in 1990. A recent poll showed that 68 percent of whites believe that 10 percent or more of all white Americans share the attitudes of the Ku Klux Klan toward Blacks. Sixty-two percent said they believe that antiblack feeling among whites has remained constant or increased in the last four or five years.

In 1965 the Kerner Commission predicted, "Our nation is moving toward two societies, one black, one white—separate and unequal." Although evidence of overt bigotry is alarming, it is arguably less significant than the facts that show the stark material reality of two nations.

A 1991 study by the U.S. Department of Housing and Urban Development, for example, reported that Blacks had more than a 50 percent chance of being discriminated against when seeking housing and that African Americans were rejected for home loans at twice the rate of whites. Study after study confirms that white and black "testers" are treated differently when they apply for housing or mortgages. We remain a largely segregated society.

According to another study, in the early 1990s more than a third of America's Blacks were living in urban ghettos, and Hispanics were similarly isolated. And while residential segregation decreases for most racial and ethnic groups with additional education, income, and occupational status, this does not hold true for African Americans.

Forty years after the Supreme Court outlawed school segregation in *Brown v. Board of Education*, racial isolation in school is still the norm for most minority children. A 1993 National School Boards Association study found that 70 percent of Black and Hispanic students now study in classrooms with a predominantly minority enrollment and that schools are becoming more segregated than ever. In the Northeast region of the country, half of Black students and 46 percent of Hispanic students attend schools where more than 90 percent of the students are minorities. These high concentrations of minority students are inevitably accompanied by the "savage inequality" of family and community poverty and sparse financial resources for the schools involved.

Stark disparities are evident when the incomes of African American and white households are compared. In 1990, for instance, the median income of African American households was 63 percent of the median income of white households. This figure was only 1 percent higher than the 62 percent in 1980, which in turn represented a 1 percent increase over the figure in 1970. In 1993 approximately 33 percent of the black population lived in poverty, compared with 13 percent of the white population. Again, there has been little change for Blacks since 1969, when about 32 percent of the Black population lived in poverty, compared with approximately 9 percent of the white population.

Disparities in incarceration and mortality rates between Blacks and whites also indicate the continuing impact of racism. Although whites are more than twice as likely as Blacks to be arrested and charged with a criminal offense, more Blacks than whites are incarcerated. Blacks below the age of seventy-five have a higher mortality rate than whites at every income level, and thirteen of the fifteen leading causes of death kill Blacks at a rate that is 10 to 54 percent higher than the rate for whites.

What is particularly disturbing is that minority children suffer from the effects of American racism even more acutely than do their parents. The poverty rate for Black children is 45 percent; for whites it is 17 percent. What's more, in 1990, 88.5 percent of all homicide victims in the United States were young African American males between the ages of fifteen and twenty-four, an increase of 10 percent over the 1980 figure.

Despite the overwhelming evidence that race continues to matter in America, many of us continue to believe that our nation has overcome its racism. The Big Lie is seductive primarily because most Americans want to believe it is true. We want to believe that we are not racists. A racist is an evil person, and most of us know that we are not cruel-hearted bigots. Moreover, if we can believe there is no racism, or that there is very little, those Americans who benefit from white privilege can continue to reap the benefits of that privilege while denying any moral responsibility for the suffering of others. Because all of the arguments against affirmative action rely on our eagerness to believe that, as a society, we are essentially free of racism, it is especially important to understand how the Big Lie works and appreciate the source of its seductiveness.

The deception begins with a rhetorical ruse that elides the ideal with reality. The constitutional ideal of equality is invoked as if equality has been achieved, so now our only concern is to guard against some new inequality, such as discrimination against white males. "Our Constitution is color-blind" we are told, as if this means that most individuals and institutions are free of racial bias. To believe this we must accept a formal and extremely narrow definition of racial discrimination or racism, under which only self-professed bigots are racists and none of us is held responsible for perpetuating the white supremacy of even the very recent past.

...

KEY WEBSITES

SOUTHERN POVERTY LAW CENTER INTELLIGENCE REPORT

The Southern Poverty Law Center, a nonprofit organization that began as a civil rights law firm in 1971, now conducts studies and informational programs on tolerance education and tracks activities of white supremacist and hate groups. Their database allows you to search for groups by type and by state. The Center's quarterly *Intelligence Report* offers in-depth analysis of political extremism and bias crimes in the United States. The *Intelligence Report* profiles Far Right leaders, monitors domestic terrorism, and reports on the activities of extremist groups. Its annual listing of hate groups is the most comprehensive in the United States. Each issue contains summaries of bias incidents from throughout the country.
**http://www.splcenter.org/cgi-bin/goframe.pl?dirname=/
intelligenceproject&pagename=ip-4.html**

RACISM AND RACE IN AMERICAN LAW

This site examines the connection between racial distinctions in the law and the role of the law in promoting/alleviating racism. It includes statutes, cases, excerpts of law review articles, annotated bibliographies, and other documents related to racism and race.
http://www.udayton.edu/~race/

RACE AND ETHNICITY RESOURCES, AMERICAN STUDIES WEB

The Race and Ethnicity Resources section is part of a comprehensive guide to American studies resources on the Internet. It contains annotated links in the following categories: African American Studies, Asian American Studies, Native American Studies, Latino and Chicano Studies, and other Race and Ethnic Resources.
http://www.georgetown.edu/crossroads/asw/race.html

BALCH INSTITUTE FOR ETHNIC STUDIES, PHILADELPHIA, PA

The Balch is a nonprofit multicultural library, archive, and educational center that works to promote intergroup relations through the preservation, collection, and representation of ethnic and immigrant histories and communities.
**http://www.ercomer.org/cgi-bin/ercomer/redir.cgi?http://
www.libertynet.org/~balch**

THE URBAN INSTITUTE, WASHINGTON, D.C., USA

The Urban Institute is a nonprofit policy research organization established in Washington, D.C., in 1968. The staff investigates the social and economic problems confronting the nation and government policies and public and

private programs designed to alleviate them. This comprehensive web site hosts many online publications.
http://www.ercomer.org/cgi-bin/ercomer/redir.cgi?http://
  www.urban.org/

MEASURING RACIAL AND ETHNIC DISCRIMINATION IN AMERICA

Michael Fix and Margery Austin Turner, "Measuring Racial and Ethnic Discrimination in America": The authors believe a National Report Card on Racial and Ethnic Discrimination is needed. Such a report card would systematize the largely haphazard, infrequent efforts to measure discrimination that have taken place in and outside government over the past fifteen years.
http://www.urban.org/civil/report_card.html